THE GRAND NATIONAL

Anne Holland has written numerous non-fiction
books relating to horse racing, including the bestselling
Steeplechasing: A Celebration, and *Best Mate: The Illustrated
Story of the Nation's Favourite Horse*. She was also a
successful amateur rider. She lives in idyllic
rural Westmeath and hunts regularly.

THE GRAND NATIONAL

THE IRISH AT AINTREE

ANNE HOLLAND

THE O'BRIEN PRESS
DUBLIN

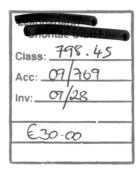
First published 2008 by The O'Brien Press Ltd,
12 Terenure Road East, Rathgar, Dublin 6, Ireland.
Tel: +353 1 4923333; Fax: +353 1 4922777
E-mail: books@obrien.ie
Website: www.obrien.ie

ISBN: 978-1-84717-074-3
Text © copyright Anne Holland 2008
Copyright for typesetting, layout, editing, design
© The O'Brien Press Ltd

A catalogue record for this title is available from the British Library

1 2 3 4 5 6 7 8
08   09   10   11   12   13

Layout and design: Anú Design, Tara
Printing: KHL, Singapore

Picture credits:

Healy Racing: front cover, all chapter openers, p vi, 2, 4, 5, 7, 8, 9, 127, 128, 132, 136, 139, 140, 142, 143, 145, 150-1, 152, 154, 157 right, 161, 162, 163, 165, 170, 174-5, 176 bottom; *Illustrated Sporting & Dramatic News:* viii & 24; Arthur Ackerman & Son Ltd. ix; Anne Holland: x top right, 48, 71, 105, 107, 146 right, 160, 164, 167, 176 top; *Illustrated London News:* xi, 12 right, 40, 62 (both), 63, 64 (bottom right); *Illustrated London News* / Mary Evans Picture Library: 19, 49, 57, 60; Courtesy of Paul Henderson: x left, 6, 76, 126, 133, 146 left, 148, 155, 157 left; Courtesy of The Topham Family Collection/Graham Budd Auctions Ltd, London: p 15, 23, 47 bottom, 59, 64 top & bottom left, 109 top left, 172; From *The Grand National* by Clive Graham & Bill Curling (Barrie & Jenkins, London 1972): 18, 51; Bridgeman Art Library: 'Earl Poulett's "The Lamb" with Mr George Ede' by Harry Hall (1814-82) Private Collection/ © Ackermann and Johnson Ltd, London, UK: 32; *Elizabeth of Bavaria* (1837-98) Winterhalter, Franz Xavier (1806-73) Kunsthistorisches Museum, Vienna, Austria: 39; Copyright © Graham Hughes / Photocall Ireland: 37; Messrs Fores, London: 47 top; Courtesy of Mr & Mrs Lenihan: 56; Courtesy of Denys Merrick: 79; *Irish Press:* 92, 94, 124; S&G/PA Photos © copyright to PA Photos and associated photographers: 97, 98; Courtesy of Joan Moore: 113, 114, 115, 116, 117; Courtesy of Niall Quaid: 149; Courtesy of Sarah Driscoll (Aintree Racecourse): 173.

Every effort has been made to trace holders of copyright material used in this book, but if any infringement of copyright has inadvertently occurred, the publishers ask the copyright holders to contact them immediately.

CONTENTS

Introduction vii

1. 2007 – *Silver Birch* I

2. In The Beginning
    1839 – The First Race; First Irish Winner, 1847 – *Mathew* II

3. Early Irish Winners
    1850-1 – *Abd El Kader*; 1855 – *Wanderer*; 1868 and 1871 – *The Lamb*;
    1879 – *The Liberator*; 1880 – *Empress* 27

4. The Beasley Connection
    1881 – *Woodbrook*; 1889 – *Frigate*; 1891 – *Come Away* 43

5. Astride The Centuries
    1895 – *Wild Man From Borneo*; 1900 – *Ambush II* 53

6. 1903 – *Drumcree* 67

7. 1920 – *Troytown*; 1939 – *Workman* 73

8. 1947 – *Caughoo* 81

9. 1953 – *Early Mist*; 1954 – *Royal Tan*; 1955 – *Quare Times* 91

10. 1958 – *Mr What* 103

11. 1975 – *L'Escargot* III

12. 1999 – *Bobbyjo* 123

13. 2000 – *Papillon* 131

14. 2003 – *Monty's Pass* 137

15. 2005 – *Hedgehunter* 147

16. 2006 – *Numbersixvalverde* 159

17. And Finally – 2008 And Beyond 169

Winners 179

Acknowledgements 187

INTRODUCTION

THE GRAND NATIONAL. The very name sends shivers down the spine. It is the world's most famous horserace. Evocative. Challenging. Romantic. The stories have come down the generations ever since the first one in 1839 when one Captain Martin Becher fell into the brook that has since borne his name. Seventeen runners turned up that day, three of them having crossed the water from Ireland with owner Tom Ferguson, setting an enduring tradition of the Irish at Aintree.

It is a race that has always fired the imagination and on which, today, many millions are staked. A worldwide audience of 600 million in 140 countries watches it live on television.

My first bet was 6d (six old pence) on *Kilmore* in 1962, ridden to victory by my hero, the great Fred Winter. To be at Aintree itself is to savour the atmosphere, to remember *Red Rum*, to be caught up in the excitement.

Once, back in the seventies, I was a tiny piece of it all, a participant in the amateur riders' hurdle on the same day. To stay in the lads' hostel overnight, to exercise at dawn alongside leading Grand National contenders, to look across at the empty stands, surrounded by green lawns, to walk the awesome course.

Later, to give refuge in the tiny make-do ladies changing room (there's a smart, purpose-built one now) to Jenny Pitman who was gasping for a fag and desperate to get away from the Press for a few moments. And that night, the empty stands again, now encircled by white from all the litter left behind.

The Grand National invariably produces a fairytale, never more so than in 2007. Almost everyone involved with 2007's winner looked like an underdog: the trainer was so raw that he had yet to train a winner at home in Ireland; the owner, a beneficiary of the

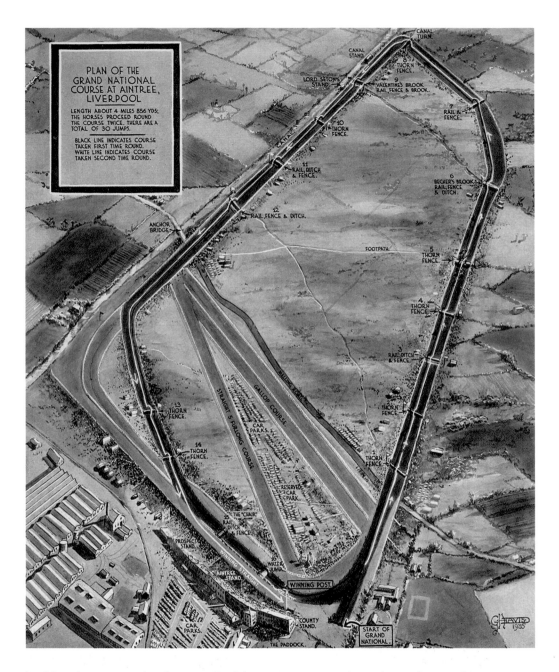

PLAN OF THE
GRAND NATIONAL
COURSE AT AINTREE,
LIVERPOOL

LENGTH ABOUT 4 MILES 856 YDS;
THE HORSES PROCEED ROUND
THE COURSE TWICE. THERE ARE A
TOTAL OF 30 JUMPS.

BLACK LINE INDICATES COURSE
TAKEN FIRST TIME ROUND.
WHITE LINE INDICATES COURSE
TAKEN SECOND TIME ROUND.

building boom in Ireland, was one of the youngest ever; the jockey, a former show-jumper, was second choice and was having only his second ride in the race; add to the mix the breeders who used to own both sire and dam but now have neither – and above all, the horse himself, *Silver Birch*: a broken down 'has been', bought cheaply, who had finished only third in a humble Westmeath point-to-point the previous winter.

No two horses have ever been trained alike for Aintree and no two stories are ever quite the same. This is part of its attraction, much of what makes it unique. That and the challenge of jumping huge fences at racing pace for more than four and a half miles. There are fairytales, heroics and heroism; there are hard luck stories, good luck stories, always stories.

Ireland, birthplace of steeple-chasing, has produced topflight racehorses since time immemorial, but in the pre-Celtic Tiger days the majority were sold abroad, mostly to England. Now there are enough Irish owners who can afford to keep horses to be trained in Ireland and the change in the results boards has been dramatic: record numbers of winners at Cheltenham and now an unprecedented six of the last ten victors of the Aintree Grand National. 2008 brought an Irish-bred and ridden winner with the second, third and fourth-placed horses all Irish-trained.

To say Ireland went through a lean spell is putting it mildly: the only Irish winner in the forty years between 1958 (*Mr What*) and 1999 (*Bobbyjo*) was *L'Escargot*, in 1975 ridden by Tommy Carberry. How poignant it was that the next Irish winner, *Bobbyjo*, was trained by Tommy and ridden by his son, Paul. Almost all of them in that period were British-bred.

Until that spell, however, more than half the Grand National winners had been Irish-bred, including a run from 1879 to 1899 in which all bar one were Irish. Irish jockeys have always been to the fore, too. It is where the horse is trained that denotes the country it represents, though, so the 1999 victory of *Bobbyjo* was very sweet. What followed was even sweeter: five more Irish victories in the next eight years, culminating in a splendid hat trick for Ireland between 2005 and 2007: *Papillon*, 2000; *Monty's Pass*, 2003; *Hedgehunter*, 2005; *Numbersixvalverde*, 2006; *Silver Birch*, 2007.

Many recall Vincent O'Brien's famous three of the 1950s, *Early Mist*, *Royal Tan* and *Quare Times*, 1953-55, but few take note that there were also three in a row from 1879-81, *The Liberator*, *Empress* and *Woodbrook*, meaning there has been one Irish hat trick for each century in which the famous race has been held. But as the one in the twenty-first century has happened so early there may be several more to come!

There are various theories on what an Aintree horse should be like, but in truth there is only one intangible quality that matters more than anything else: heart. After that comes ability, agility, jumping prowess, stamina, class. There have been tiny winners: *The Lamb* and *Abd El Kader* both of whom won twice in the nineteenth century were tiny horses. *Battleship*, 1938, and *Caughoo*, 1947, were both about 15.2 hands; *Team Spirit*, 1964, was only 15 hands high.

Above all, there is the 'Aintree factor'. Some horses simply take to the place, rise to the challenge, and thrive on the occasion. Agility, the ability to find a 'fifth leg' is what *Red Rum* – bred to be a sprinter – had in abundance.

Red Rum, Manifesto, Mr What, Corbiere, West Tip, and more recently, *Hedgehunter*, were horses who not only won, but who came back bouncing for more. Others do not. A surprising number of winners have fallen at the first fence the next year, *Aldaniti, Hallo Dandy, Poethyln*, to name a few; some simply 'don't want to know' a second time. But there are those, not quite good enough to win, who will run well year after year, often running into a place, always consistent: *Tiberetta, Wyndburgh, Freddie, Greasepaint, Durham Edition, Suny Bay* are some examples.

The Grand National is one of the few sporting events of the world to be known to all, across the board. There are thousands of otherwise non-racing people who hold a passion for the Grand National. For millions more it is simply their annual flutter.

The Grand National gets into the blood; this can happen to someone totally unconnected with horses, let alone one who owns, trains or rides them. For academic John Pinfold it began when he was standing by the Canal Turn in 1967, aged fourteen. It was pouring with rain and there was a religious zealot standing on a soapbox in front of the crowd proclaiming that they were all sinners and must find God. He then mentioned that he had been a Liverpool policeman and with that the crowd swept forward, picked him up and threw him over the fence on to the canal towpath. It was that year that mayhem was caused by a loose horse at the fence before the Canal Turn when only one runner, *Foinavon*, got over at the first attempt. John was hooked.

Tim Cox from Surrey houses a collection of thirteen thousand racing books, and print material; he aims to produce a complete listing of all books published on the thoroughbred horse on his website, www.thecoxlibrary.com; Chris Simpson from Kent has titled his website www.freewebs.com/grandnationalanorak. Both gentlemen enjoy sharing their knowledge with anyone who logs on while another buff, Mick Mutlow, recalls as a twelve-year-old watching a race on television with 'big green obstacles' won by a certain horse called *Red Rum*. Mick, a factory works manager in Essex, would win any Mastermind competition on the Grand National, yet, amazingly, he has never been to a race meeting, let alone the National.

For Jane Clarke from Essex her obsession with the race led to her becoming curator of the burgeoning Aintree museum. In November 2007, on behalf of Lord Daresbury, Aintree chairman, she bought back the Aintree Racecourse mounting bell that was in an auction by Tophams of Aintree memorabilia. The guide price was £3,000-£5,000 but she had to go to £9,000 to secure it – and had it back and hung at Aintree to be rung in time for the November Becher meeting, thus continuing a tradition going back to 1831, pre-dating the National itself.

Aintree on Grand National day is an experience to be savoured, gradually watching the empty stands filling up, the Liver girls arriving in their flimsy dresses and high-heeled sandals mingling with the tweed-suited, the almost tangible atmosphere building up to the great race.

To be there. To be a part of it all. The magic never palls.

2007 – SILVER BIRCH

IT IS 7AM ON SATURDAY, 14 APRIL 2007. A thin sun breaks through the low mist hanging over Aintree Racecourse; this mist heralds a cloudless, sunny, warm day for the world's most famous race. In the distance, the empty stands tower over the manicured grass sward that is the finishing straight. The last of the watering ended at 1 am leaving perfect going. Flowers surround the finishing post, the paddock, the marquees, and *Red Rum*'s statue. Look the other way and in the distance unprepossessing skyscrapers, chimneys and pylons rise beyond the furthest fence, the Canal Turn. In the in-field is the old motor racing circuit. The last British Grand Prix at Aintree was in 1962, but the track has been used over the years for minor events and today motor-cycle meetings are held on a few weekends a year. There can never again be car racing on the full circuit as the new stands encroach on to the original track. Instead, it is more likely to be occupied by Pony Club members at summer camp.

Now, on Grand National morning, the stable lads' hostel is already empty, bar the canteen staff busily preparing breakfast for the lads and lasses to return to. Some of the horses are

out on the turf, the great and the would-be great mingling with the merely moderate, enjoying their pre-race fresheners, walking, trotting, cantering, some in company, others alone. More hopefuls are being tended to in their stables; the doors of some bear name-plates of previous Grand National winners that were housed behind them.

Will last year's winner, *Numbersixvalverde*, or the previous victor, *Hedgehunter*, score again, to make a hat trick for Ireland? *Hedgehunter's* trainer, Willie Mullins, has three more in the race: Thyestes Chase winner *Homer Wells*, outsider *Livingstonebramble*, and the quietly fancied *Bothar Na*. Tom Taaffe has *Slim Pickings*, *Cloudy Bays* runs for Charles Byrnes, and Ted Walsh runs former Troytown Chase winner *Jack High*. And there are high hopes for *Point Barrow*, former Irish National winner and mount of Philip Carberry. Money is piling on for him and for the English-trained *Monkerhostin* who looks all over a National type, as well as former Scottish National winner *Joes Edge*. *Dun Doire* is trained by Tony Martin for the Dunderry syndicate headed by Barry Callaghan of Capranny, Trim, County Meath. He has leased the stables there to a young, newly-licensed trainer. One of its occupants is another Irish runner in the big race, *Silver Birch*. He used to be good. He won a Becher Chase at Aintree and a Welsh National for Paul Nicholls, and was ante-post favourite for the 05 National, but he was off the course for more than a year with leg trouble and lost his way. He ran in the 2006 Grand National, but fell at the Chair and was pulled up in two races before that, so he was sent to the Sales. Now he's with this young trainer who has yet to train a winner in his home country (but has crossed the water for two victories in Perth and one in Newton Abbott).

Silver Birch's role in life these days is to contend cross-country races. To be a fun horse. No pressure. The hunting he enjoyed this winter was fun, too. A natural. Jumped the infamous Culmullen Double out with the Wards (the famous Ward Union Staghounds). Not a bother.

His twenty-nine-year-old trainer, Gordon Elliott, is aboard him now in the early morning light. The horse is so eager that afterwards his rider's arms feel a few inches longer from struggling to restrain him. He looks well, bouncing. That good second in the Cheltenham Festival's cross-country race has left him spot on.

No posh hotel for Gordon, he has slept in the hostel. He'll meet the even younger owner, Brian Walsh, later. Fiona Dowling, who hails from Kerry, gets on with plaiting *Silver Birch*, the bay by *Clearly Bust*. Breeders Joe and Mel Power are at home in Cork, but will be watching 'their' boy on the telly. *Clearly Bust* only sired about seventy foals before dying in an accident, and the Powers sold the dam, *All Gone*, in 2000. A promising full-brother to *Silver Birch* broke a leg in a point-to-point. But the couple don't dwell on bad luck. They're shortly to bask in pride.

Fiona Dowling used to work for Gordon, but is now a student at the Irish National Stud. The stud has given her a dispensation to travel with the horse and she makes a perfect job of preparing him; his plaits are neat and his coat glistens in the sunshine. Gordon walks the 4½-mile course three times, firstly with 'the lads' from Trim, then with his pal, jockey Jason Maguire, and then yet once more. *Silver Birch*'s price goes out from 25-1 to 33s.

'It would have been half that if he was still with Paul Nicholls,' Gordon readily admits.

He has been at the course since Thursday, and had a runner, *Fable*, in the Foxhunters, the 'amateurs National'. Ridden by his brother, Joey, he gets round safely to finish tenth.

Now the forty runners are parading in the paddock. Jockey Robbie Power, wearing the owner's black and light blue starred colours, joins Gordon Elliott and Brian Walsh, and his girlfriend, Karen. The antique paddock bell goes, and Fiona holds on to the horse as the jockey is legged up into the saddle. Gordon had hoped his best friend Jason Maguire would ride, but he has picked the fancied *Idle Talk* instead. Robbie, who won a silver medal for Ireland as a junior show-jumper, will be an able substitute. His father, Con, was a leading international show-jumper, part of the Irish team that won and then earned the right to keep the country's most prestigious trophy, the Aga Khan Cup, through three consecutive annual wins for it at the Royal Dublin Show. Robbie and his event rider sister Elizabeth inherited their father's winning attitude; Robbie rode eleven winners in his first season racing. Pictures of him on a Shetland pony as a tiny boy show he already had a 'racing' seat. His grandfather, also Con, bred 1947 Grand National winner *Caughoo*.

Now the jockeys are mounting. No less than twenty-four of the horses are Irish bred. Eleven were bred in France, just four in the UK and one, *Zabenz*, in New Zealand. Well over half the jockeys are Irish.

But no one is thinking too much about nationalities as at last (after a few attempts) the tapes ping up and they're off to the traditional roar of the crowd.

At the very first fence the dreams of *Point Barrow*'s supporters crash. *The Outlier* and then *Naunton Brook* skip along merrily in the lead until heading out on the final circuit.

Gordon Elliott finds himself standing next to Helen Walsh, wife of Ted, whose *Jack High* falls at the first Becher's; the horse gets up, and Helen lends her binoculars to Gordon. *Livingstonebramble* also goes down there, and *Monkerhostin* calls it a day one fence later, the seventh, clearly being one of those to take a dislike to the place. *Cloudy Bays* follows suit at The Chair.

They're on the second circuit now, and *Idle Talk* dislodges Jason Maguire at the nineteenth. *Simon* is running a cracking race for Mercy Rimell whose late husband, Fred, trained four Grand National winners, and the mare, *Liberthine*, is running a blinder for amateur Sam Waley-Cohen, whose own Aintree record is impeccable.

They're approaching Becher's for the second time. *Bewleys Berry*, going well, has taken over

the lead, but crumples here. *Silver Birch* and Robbie Power, taking the 'brave man's route' down the inside (where the drops are steeper), cleverly avoid the fallen rider, compatriot Paddy Brennan. *Graphic Approach* is another to fall here and *Liberthine* is left in the lead.

At the Canal Turn *Ballycassidy* and Denis O'Regan, still near the front after being hampered at Becher's, finally give way to gravity. *Hedgehunter* and *Numbersixvalverde* are still there but can't make enough headway; *Joe's Edge* is tailed off, *Homer Wells*, *Dun Doire* and *Bothar Na* can't go with the leaders and are also pulled up.

But a few are making steady headway as they approach the Canal Turn for the last time. Tom Taaffe's *Slim Pickings* is one of them. *McKelvey* is another, and also 100-1 shot *Philson Run*, while the mare, *Liberthine*, is still there. And with them is *Silver Birch*. His colours can be seen moving into second place after the third-last fence.

Gordon returns the binoculars to Helen. His hands are shaking too much to see through them. They're approaching the last. Only *Slim Pickings* is ahead of *Silver Birch*. *Silver Birch* is foot perfect and jumps into the lead as his rival makes a mistake. Now that long, long, infamous run-in, past the elbow, and *McKelvey* is closing, he's getting nearer, nearer – but not near enough. *Silver Birch* strides past the post three-quarters of a length clear. The 'has-been', the forgotten horse of the Irish XI, has made it three in a row for Ireland.

'My dream was to win the Grand National. That was *the* race for me, more than the Cheltenham Gold Cup,' admits twenty-six-year-old Brian Walsh.

So, now that he has succeeded at his first attempt the goal that others endeavour to achieve throughout a lifetime, what next? To win it again, of course! And again …

The son of Kilcock farmers Brian and Caroline Walsh, Brian junior inherited some nearby land as the result of helping and keeping an eye on the elderly owner, and sold it for development. His is a real 'new Ireland' story. He now lives in a purpose-built stud named Rheindross, after his first winner on the track, housing twenty mares divided between flat and National Hunt. The flat mares are in foal to the likes of *Galileo* and *Johannesburg*.

'Well, I only want the best,' Brian reasons, though he enjoys jumping most.

He has about twelve horses in training, some with Charlie Mann in England, three or four with Paul Nolan in Wexford or Paul Gilligan in Galway, some for the flat with Karl Burke in the UK – and, of course, *Silver Birch* with Gordon Elliott, bought at Doncaster Sales for £20,000, but with enough past form to ensure a 'racing weight' in the National, that is, to ensure he will be handicapped high enough to get into the race; many low weights fall below the maximum of forty runners allowed to take part and therefore cannot run. The purchase tag looks very little now.

In his first two or three years as an owner Brian has tasted early success, notably in the Summer National at Uttoxter in 2005 with *Rheindross*. He had a share in a Grand National runner, *Good Shuil*, who pulled up in the 2003 race won by *Monty's Pass*.

Both Brian's runners at the 2007 Cheltenham Festival finished second, *Silver Birch* in the cross-country race and *Air Force I*, trained by Charlie Mann, in the Brit Insurance Novices Hurdle.

It was *Silver Birch*'s Cheltenham performance that persuaded Brian not only to let him

take his chance in the National, but also convinced him that he had a chance. Nevertheless, it was intended as a stepping stone for the premier cross-country race, the La Touche, at Ireland's National Hunt Festival in Punchestown, and then possibly a crack at the Velka Parducbice, the extraordinary, highly challenging 'Czech Grand National' the following autumn. Instead, *Silver Birch* found himself parading at Punchestown and the Curragh as Ireland's latest hero.

Brian Walsh was always interested in racing, and after he 'came into a few quid' he was able to indulge his dreams. He is one of those few to have seen his dreams come true. And who knows, there really could be repeat performances.

Gordon Elliott, a former amateur jockey, for all his inexperience as a trainer, nevertheless had had the perfect tuition with Martin Pipe, where he also rode a winner from just six rides. And before that with Tony Martin, one of Ireland's shrewdest trainers. And right at the beginning with Martin Lynch.

As a small boy, Gordon and his sisters and cousins were taken to the local point-to-points by two uncles, and that was enough to sow a small seed. One day, when he was about ten years old, Gordon's parents Pat and Jane sent him from their Summerhill, County Meath, home to deliver a message to Martin Lynch, something to do with a car. He ended

up hosing a horse's leg for the former jockey turned trainer, and the next thing was that he was there every day after school. Martin's wife, Suzanne, taught him to ride on a pony and by the time he was a teenager he had moved on to be working weekends and holidays at trainer Tony Martin's, riding work and eventually being given one or two rides in races.

Soon it was a case of,

'I was to be kicked out of school or leave, so I left.'

By now Gordon had caught the racing bug; he rode nearly two hundred winners in all, the majority in point-to-points, and he only stopped race-riding a year before the National victory when he repeatedly dislocated his shoulders. He also twice rode in the Maryland Hunt Cup, the American timber race where some of the solid fences are five feet high. Naturally quite big, the battle with the scales was another problem, so he took out a restricted licence and trained mostly point-to-pointers, gradually running more under Rules, especially in England where 'there are weaker races and there is less balloting out', the latter being the current scourge of Irish racing, a victim of its own success. Put simply, there are too many horses for the number of races and meetings in a year to go round; courses have a safety limit of so many runners per race (more on a wide track, less on a narrow one); so if, say, seventy horses are declared for a race where a maximum of twenty is allowed, fifty will be balloted out. He received his full licence a matter of days before the Grand National, and three weeks later he had a win in Kilbeggan, his first win in an Irish race, quickly following that up with a win in Down Royal, Northern Ireland. Six months after his National win Gordon's inmates had doubled in number and include one that may have a crack at the Champion Hurdle, and another bought specifically with the Maryland Hunt Cup in mind for an American owner. Sadly, it was also announced that *Silver Birch* would not be defending his crown, due to a little heat in a foreleg, so it was decided not to risk training him for 2008; however, it's hoped that he'll be fit for another crack at winning the Grand National again in 2009.

After *Silver Birch*'s win the first to congratulate Gordon on his fantastic achievement were father and son, Martin and David Pipe. Paul Nicholls, former trainer of *Silver Birch*, was close behind – and the champion British trainer admitted he would not have won the race with him. It was the small yard, the change of scene, and above all the hunting that had transformed him. His temperament behind hounds had proved superb, and his prowess at jumping whatever came in the way – big ditch, huge bank, high rails, gate – had shown him to be a natural.

'It helped him mentally, sweetened him up,' Gordon says. 'He was top class.'

Months after the win Gordon was, unsurprisingly, still enjoying it, 'living the dream'.

That's what the Grand National is all about.

2

IN THE BEGINNING

1839 – THE FIRST RACE; FIRST IRISH WINNER, 1847 – MATHEW

RIGHT FROM THE START AINTREE PULLED IN THE CROWDS, thanks to an entrepreneur capable of making it all happen. William Lynn ran the Waterloo Hotel, close to where Liverpool's Central Station is now, with aplomb and when he instigated a hare-coursing event known as the Waterloo Cup he discovered that combatants would travel from far and wide to take part, increasing his hotel trade admirably. The event tested the prowess of greyhounds to the utmost and The Cup became – and remained – the most sought after accolade in the coursing world.

If a comparatively minority sport could do that for William Lynn's trade, what about the world of horse racing? Flat racing took place locally on Lord Sefton's land at Aintree, but the newfangled steeple-chasing was catching on elsewhere; for five years there had been a prestigious event at St Alban's, and nearby Maghull had got in on the act, too. Indeed, some sources claim the Grand National began there in 1837, the year Queen Victoria ascended the throne, but newspaper reports show that Maghull closed in 1834. A

majority verdict puts the inaugural running of the great race as the one at Aintree in 1839, although local newspaper reports show that it began there in 1836; it only attracted a few runners in 1837 and 38 – when it was won for Ireland by Alan McDonough riding *Sir William* – and was then revamped, repackaged and re-launched as the Grand Liverpool Steeplechase with a great deal of what today is called 'spin' in 1839. As the 1836 race was a 'seller' (the lowest class of race, after which the winner is auctioned), it may still be best to refer to that as a forerunner, rather than the actual thing.

Flat racing had taken place at Aintree for a decade – Lord Molyneux placed a bottle full of sovereigns in the footings of the grandstand opened on 7 February 1829. The *Liverpool Chronicle* of February 14 recorded that, 'a small crowd of about forty gentlemen, some respectable pedestrians, watched Lord Molyneux lay the foundation of the new Grandstand. Beneath it he deposited some coins of the realm, and then spread the mortar over it using a silver trowel. Afterwards the gentlemen partook of a cold collation prepared for the occasion by Lynn, and success to the Liverpool Races was toasted in bumpers of sparkling champagne, whilst the workmen were treated to an ample allowance of beer and spirits.'

It was in 1835 that Lynn introduced hurdle races, followed a year later by the new chase, later to be known as the Grand National, won by Captain Martin Becher on *The Duke* (or *The Iron Duke*). In that year, 1836, Lynn held two days of coursing, followed by the day of racing, then concluding with another day's coursing. The new chase became a handicap in 1843; from 1841 some newspapers had dubbed it the Liverpool Grand National

Steeplechase. When the title was altered to The Liverpool and National Steeplechase, and it was in 1847 that the words 'Grand National' appeared for the first time, with all sources at the time and ever since recognising it as that.

Having failed to attract St Alban's Chase runners for those first three years, William Lynn was nearly bankrupt; he sold one hundred shares to the nobility and gentry for £25 each, which resulted in it being run by a committee and reduced his influence on it but this could be called the first rescue of the race – there were many 'last' Grand Nationals in the 1960s and 70s when it looked as if the land would be sold for development until a Jockey Club package, with support from funds raised by the public, finally rescued it for posterity in 1983.

Word of the 1839 race had spread far and wide; 'spin' was plentiful, and all roads led to Aintree. Thus William Lynn was the single founder of two of country sports' most enduring pinnacles. The sad thing is that he died penniless and lies in an unmarked grave, plot 299a that cost £2 16/-, while the great race that he founded boasts an annual turnover of some £34 million. But he is not forgotten. Sir Mark Prescott, Newmarket Flat trainer and coursing-lover extraordinaire, restored Lynn's grave and used to leave flowers on it every year on his way to the Waterloo Cup, sadly no longer run since anti-hunting legislation in 2004.

Tuesday, February 26, 1839 saw an original entry of more than fifty-three for the Grand Liverpool Steeplechase reduced to eighteen on the day, but one, *Jerry* (who was to win in 1840), was withdrawn because his owner was unable to find a suitable jockey at the weight, so seventeen faced the starter. Although run on the same site as today, it looked very different then: it was farmland, much of it plough, and the riders could 'take their own line' across the natural country; fences were not individually marked, there were simply a few flags en route to indicate the general direction.

The roads towards the village three miles outside of Liverpool were clogged as people from all ranks made their way, on horseback, by coach, brougham, trap and cart; steamer, gig and wagon – and many more by foot, some 30-40,000 in all, according to contemporary reports. From Scotland, Wales, Ireland and all parts of England they came. Ticket touts, prostitutes, drunks; purveyors of 'fast food'; cigar sellers, card sharks, swindlers and pick-pockets all had a field day. Horse-drawn omnibuses were so full that offers of half a guinea (52½ pence) for the 2/6d (12½p) ride were turned down. The Liverpool hotels and board-ing hotels were so oversubscribed that some rooms were let four to a bed. Lynn's Waterloo Hotel and the still famous Adelphi (scene of many Grand National high-jinks and numerous celebrations over the years) each let a hundred beds. Everyone in the sporting world was talking about the forthcoming race, and all this before the advent of the telephone – let alone mobile phones, the internet, or television! Even the hunting swells, who still considered their sport superior to merely chasing distant steeples from point to point, came to watch, and, dressed in their finery, filled the fine houses.

This new race was all the talk. Its rules were that it was for 'gentleman' riders over four miles across country, a sweepstake of 20 sovereigns each, 100 added; no rider allowed to 'open a gate or ride through a gateway, or more than 100 yards along any road, footpath or drift-way.' The actual course was probably revealed to the jockeys shortly before the race.

Irishman Tom Ferguson must have been confident enough that his journey would be worth his while to cross the water with three runners, *Daxon, Barkston* and *Rust.* Tom already had experience of Aintree, having travelled over the previous July for the Tradesman's Cup with a good horse, *Harkaway.* He trained from Rossmore Lodge on the Curragh and he has been described both as 'eccentric' and 'bucolic'. Now his three runners were either walked or taken in an 'iron horse' carriage (a train) to the Dublin docks and loaded onto a ferry in which they most probably endured, in February, a rough crossing. On reaching Liverpool docks they had to travel about five miles to the course, in all likelihood mingling with the vast crowds already making their way there.

The day of the race dawned clear, but the ground was deep, and much of it was plough. Tom chose to ride *Daxon* himself, Larry Byrne, who was shortly after to succeed Ferguson at Rossmore, was on *Barkston* and William McDonough had what was to prove a rather startling ride on *Rust.* Tom Ferguson might be bringing three horses across the water from Ireland, but he was going to find keen competition from the home side.

Among their rivals was Mr John Elmore's *Lottery,* to be ridden by 'Dandy' Jem Mason, and Captain Childe's *Conrad* to be ridden by Captain Martin Becher. John Elmore was one of those to set his sights on the big new chase at Aintree and, leaving no stone unturned, he sent *Lottery* to the Epsom yard of George Dockeray, trainer of the Derby winner *Lapdog.* There, the speedy flat racers found they could not get away from the raw-boned, half-bred chaser, *Lottery.*

Sartorially foppish 'Dandy' Mason may have been, but his outwardly fey looks hid nerves of steel, a will of iron, and an outstanding horseman of the day. He had twice ridden *Lottery* in the St Alban's, but the first time his saddle had slipped and in 1838 the horse was 'amiss'. But he won an important steeplechase in Barnet in 'a common canter' and then caused a minor sensation by beating Captain Becher on his great *Vivian* at Daventry, Northamptonshire.

Martin Becher (1797-1864) was renowned for his steeplechasing wins on *Vivian,* a stallion bought in Dublin for 16 guineas. In 1834 he won a £1,000 match on him against Lord Henry, third Marquis of Waterford, at Market Harborough, Leicestershire.

He served abroad for three years with the army of occupation after the Napoleonic Wars. He began racing in 1823 and was one of the first great steeplechase riders. As a boy he learnt to ride all sorts of horses and ponies; when he left school he was stationed in Brussels at the time of Waterloo in the Store-keeping General's Department. When he returned to Norfolk he broke and trained many horses and rode in races all over the country, once travelling a then astonishing seven hundred miles in two weeks. He served as a Commissioned Officer in the Buckinghamshire Yeomanry and did duty near Westminster Abbey at the Coronation of George IV, for which he earned a medal. Once back, he made friends with Thomas Coleman who had renamed his inn near St Alban's the Turf Hotel and, like Linde who was to follow, began filling it with racing visitors – and plenty of 'craic'!

It is said that Captain Becher had a 'kindly, rugged face, with small, bright penetrating eyes'; thickset and shrewd, he had a 'bushy beard and thick grey locks' and there was something 'very resolute and vigorous about his bearing' even in old age.

The son of a Norfolk farmer, his roots were Irish. His ancestor, Mr Henry Wrixon of Ballygiblin, County Cork, was Master of the Duhallow hounds in 1745, the oldest pack of foxhounds in Ireland; the next Master was Henry Wrixon's son, Colonel William Wrixon, followed by his son, Sir William Wrixon Becher, who resigned in 1822. (His grandson, Mr W. Norton Barry, was to be Master from 1886-93).

Going back to an even further ancestor, at the Battle of the Boyne in 1690, King William's aide-de-camp was Colonel Thomas Becher. At the end of the battle, the King asked his aide-de-camp the time; Becher was unable to answer him and King William presented his own watch to him. Nearly 320 years later, the watch is still with a branch of the Becher family.

Now at last it was almost time for the first Grand National to begin. It was to produce drama, excitement, death, publicity, stories; all the familiar ingredients of today were there from the start.

The course began on the far side of Moss Lane (now called Melling Road) and the first fence was a high bank, part of it topped with rails, and part with gorse and hawthorn. Fence three was described as a 'horrendous' ditch five feet wide with a timber fence on the take-off side. From there the runners ran through a field of wheat, jumped a high bank, and then approached one of the biggest fences, the first of the three brook fences. This Brook Number 1 (so called for that year only) consisted of firstly a timber fence, 4 feet 2 inches high, then a stump hedge and next a ditch five or six feet wide with a natural brook running through it, beyond which the landing (substantially lower than the take-off side) was on a steepish grassy bank. The total spread of this obstacle was between 17 and 18 feet.

After proceeding over more grass fields divided by small hedges, the line of country then took a sharp left turn over a ploughed field, the jump out of which was the second brook fence. Only twenty yards further on from the previous fence and close to the canal, this consisted of firstly a rail, followed by a small hedge, and beyond this was a parallel ditch filled with water (purposely filled for racing) about nine to ten feet in width. The landing side of this obstacle was three feet lower than the take off side in some places, and was made difficult by the spongy nature of the soil upon landing. The total spread of this leap was close to twenty-four feet, and was to become Valentine's Brook.

The next obstacles were the two leaps either side of Moss Lane, near the Canal Bridge at the north-east corner of the course; the first jump (into the lane) was unimportant, but the leap out of the lane, (a hedge) was more difficult. Here riders had the option instead of jumping a five-barred gate, or a piece of railing which made up a gap in the hedge, bordered on the take off side by a deep ditch. Once over, the landing level here was in some places four feet above the take-off side, resembling a table, by which name it was known for a while in the late 1870s.

The runners then proceeded onto the training ground (inside of the racecourse) and the next obstacle, opposite the grandstand, was a temporary but strong wall, about five feet high and topped with turf.

The line of country then took the runners to the south end of the course, to Moss Lane again. Here the hedge on the grandstand side of Moss Lane was razed to the ground to give the horses a clear leap over a ditch. Once in the lane the runners then had to clear a high hedge that was five feet in most places, but in some parts eight feet high, to get into the field beyond.

The remaining fences, intermittently encountered between the big ones, were mostly small hedges. Nevertheless, then as now, the race was not for the faint-hearted. In succeeding years a number of posts and rails were erected to make the race even more of a jumping test, but that first year it was mainly natural country.

One thing happened before the first Grand National that would be unthinkable today. A horse called *The Nun* was found to be 'too fat', and was promptly taken off for a two-mile gallop before the race could begin. Irishman Allen McDonough, brother of William, rode her. Betting played a big part then as now – there was a large gambling tent erected on the course – and there was plenty of money for *Daxon* and *Rust* from Ireland, for *Charity* and, towards the off, for *Lottery* who started favourite. By this time not only were the stands full, but also most of the trees had been climbed by the young and agile. Many more mounted spectators galloped all over the place looking for vantage viewing spots and, in trying to keep up with the action, no doubt jumped some of the fences as well. Some spectators watched from beside the Liverpool and Leeds Canal that skirts the long stretch from the 'Canal Turn' back towards home via Valentines and the Melling road; even more spectators gathered around the brooks looking for a splashing. They were not to be disappointed.

When the starter finally dropped his flag for the horses to set off for the first 'Grand National' he could never have envisaged that there would be 600 million people world-wide watching the latest renewal 170 years later.

Once off and running it was Irishman Tom who led the way on *Daxon*, with Captain Becher in close attendance on *Conrad*. As they headed out into the country towards Brook No 1, Tom was unaware that another of his runners, *Rust*, had been trapped by a mob and held in a laneway on the first circuit, in the vicinity of where the Anchor Bridge is now. He was going too well for the crowd whose money was on another horse so they virtually kidnapped him, surrounding him, possibly hanging on to his bridle. By the time they let him go it was too late to catch up, and he was eventually pulled up.

The remaining runners approached the first brook, an extremely challenging obstacle, not only in height and width, but also with the big drop on landing to catch out the unwary. Making it even trickier was the fact that it was jumped out of deep plough. Tom Ferguson had Martin Becher breathing down his neck as they galloped towards it, probably too fast. *Daxon* hit the rails hard and somehow retained his feet on landing, but *Conrad*, close behind, fell, sending Captain Becher into orbit. The rest of the field was following, so, taking evasive action, Becher plunged into the brook for safety until the rest had soared over. He is quoted as saying that he never knew water tasted so foul without whiskey in it. (Or brandy, depending on the version of the story told).

Local reports say that Becher caught his horse, remounted and galloped so hard after the remainder that he actually took the lead. But the effort was too much in such heavy conditions and *Conrad* fell again, this time galloping off loose and evading recapture. *Daxon* was also remounted after a fall later in the course and then fell again, and he, too, galloped off loose. The lead was now held by *Charity*, followed by *Lottery*, *Railroad* and *Jack*.

As they neared the end of the first circuit they were faced with the biggest obstacle of all, the pile of stones nearly five foot high, situated in front of the grandstand. The surprise here was that the one faller was *Charity*, the mare from the Cotswolds, where she had been trained to jump over the many walls. She was to redeem herself two years later. Two more fell at Brook No 2, *The Nun*, who was remounted and finished fifth, and Mr J.S. Oswell's *Dictator*, who suffered a broken back and died.

Now the final shape of the race showed *Lottery* to be going easily, and as he approached the last upright rails it was all over bar a fall. He did not disappoint, putting in a prodigious leap said to be 33 feet, and becoming the appropriately named first winner.

In all, nine of the seventeen runners fell (although some reports put *Charity* as having refused), with just poor *Rust* being given as pulled up.

From that day on, the Grand National was forever the greatest steeplechase. It had its detractors, too, for with a fatality in the first running there were those who claimed the course was too severe, causing outcry in the Press. *Plus ça change.*

Lottery's time was slow by today's standards, but the runners had to contend with deep plough and there is no doubt that he was a very good horse. After Aintree he won races at Cheltenham, Stratford, Maidstone and Dunchurch; it was said he could trot faster than most could gallop! He was deemed so good that the handicapper and the race programmers gave him the sort of burdens and restrictions that were not to be seen again for another one and a quarter centuries until a certain horse named *Arkle* came along …

◆ ◆ ◆

It was to be eight years before Ireland recorded its first official win in the National, with a horse called *Mathew*, in 1847.

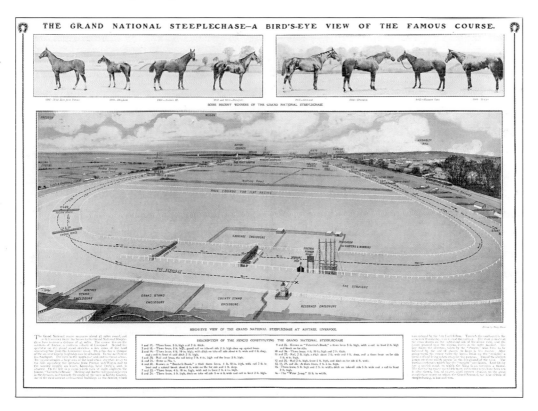

THE GRAND NATIONAL STEEPLECHASE—A BIRD'S-EYE VIEW OF THE FAMOUS COURSE.

Before that, in 1840 half the field of thirteen had come from Ireland, fired no doubt by Tom Ferguson's tales of derring-do the previous year. One of the Irish runners was *Valentine*, owned and ridden by Alan Power. He laid a bet that he would be first over the wall, and so he set off at breakneck speed, far too fast for the fences, but he survived as far as Brook number 2. There, meeting it all wrong, *Valentine* tried to refuse, but was going at such a speed that sheer momentum saw him corkscrew his way over: somehow horse and rider stayed together – and on they galloped towards the wall. *Valentine* was weakening and *Lottery* was gaining on him with every stride, but Power just managed to get there first – only to hear the sound of stones crumbling as *Lottery* and two others fell behind him. As for Brook no 2, it was forever afterwards dubbed 'Valentines'. *Jerry*, trained by George Dockeray came in first; *Arthur* was second and *Valentine* got round to finish third, with compatriot the sporting Marquis of Waterford taking fourth and last place on *The Sea*. His other runner, *Columbine*, fell, as did most of the remaining runners.

Henry Waterford had been a spirited pupil at Eton where he earned accolades in boxing and rowing, but it was in the hunting field and on the turf that he spent most of his time as a young adult in England, riding in his first steeplechase at Aylesbury in 1834. He did not race in Ireland until 1841 but the following year laid out a course on his own land at what is now New Inn, between Cahir and Cashel in County Tipperary. In that same year he also bought the Tipperary hounds and showed fine sport. In January 1843 the hounds

killed outside the walls of Thomastown Castle, birthplace of Father Theobald Mathew, of whom more shortly.

Waterford kept trying to get his colours of blue jacket, black cap first past the Grand National post, although he did not ride in the race himself again. *Columbine* failed to complete the course in 1842; the next year, the first as a handicap, his *Redwing* refused in the race won by *Vanguard,* and in 1846 his *Regalia* fell. It was to be 1850 before he tried again when his *Sir John* was third, as he was the next year also. In 1852 he had two runners, *Warner* was sixth and *Sir John* seventh; he had 'also rans' in 1853 and 1854, and a faller in 1859.

Tom Ferguson also tried again, in 1842, and like Waterford, did not ride again. His *Banathlath*, ridden by a jockey named Peter Colgan, fell in the race won by *Lottery*'s owner, Mr Elmore, with *Gaylad*, ridden by 'Black Tom' Olliver; Colgan remounted and *Banathlath* finished in fifth place. Poor *Lottery* was still carrying 18 lb more than anyone else for having won the Cheltenham Steeplechase two years previously; even so he started favourite, but was pulled up by Jem Mason.

The year 1847 was a black one for Ireland, much of which was in the grip of famine and

death caused by failed potato harvests; in some quarters, not dependent upon the potato for survival, life continued much as before: balls in Dublin, exports on the docks – and Irish runners in Aintree. For the first time, an Irish trained horse won the Grand National: *Mathew*, almost certainly named after the abstinence pioneer, Father Theobald Mathew.

The first Irish anti-drink societies had appeared in the late 1820s; they were dominated by urban, middle-class Protestants and were directed against the consumption of spirits by the working classes. Catholic total abstinence societies emerged in the 1830s. Such societies were also taking hold in England where the Catholic population had dwindled to barely 100,000 at the end of the eighteenth-century. Catholic emancipation helped it revive and with mass Irish immigration during the famine, it grew to a quarter of a million; this was the time when the Roman Catholic Church in England became involved in charity work, often in trying to curb drink-dependence.

In Ireland, Father Theobald Mathew founded his society in Cork in 1829; it proved to be the most successful of them all and by the early 1840s its membership was said to run into millions.

Theobald 'Toby' Mathew, 1790-1856, was born in Thomastown Castle near Golden, County Tipperary. Huge and turreted, the castle was originally a pink brick two-storey longhouse built in 1670 for George Mathew, half brother to the Great Duke of Ormonde. Judicious marriages meant the family grew richer and various additions and improvements were made in 1711 including a 50-foot long dining room that faced the Galtee Mountains, with the park, avenues and formal gardens in between. In 1812 Francis Mathew obtained the services of Sir Richard Morrison to transform it into a multi-turreted castle, and refaced the exterior in concrete that was painted a pale blue. The Mathew family was famous for its 'high living, hospitality and self-indulgence' and uninvited guests were made welcome, almost as if it were a hotel. Although they outwardly conformed to the Established Church it was believed they remained closet Catholics. The young Toby was sent to St Patrick's College, Maynooth, to study for the priesthood, but when he gave a party in his rooms he was given the choice of leaving or being expelled; he left. Later he joined the Capuchin order, and was posted to Cork, where he ministered to the poor and organised instruction for children.

A man of strength and character, he more and more saw the degradation wrought by spirit drinking, and although he enjoyed whiskey punch himself, he was eventually persuaded to found the Cork Total Abstinence Society, supposedly with the words, 'Here goes, in the name of God'.

His success was sensational; his preaching of temperance as a cure-all for Ireland's problems won massive support with millions taking the pledge, especially during the 1830s. Sales of spirits halved and the movement was described as 'a mighty moral miracle'. By 1845, with the Great Famine taking hold, he expended much of his energy on securing help for the afflicted, through providing soup kitchens and persuading the British to allow

food imports. In 1847, the year of racehorse *Mathew*'s Aintree success, the priests in Cork selected him to be their bishop, but it was opposed by other bishops (because he had sought help from the British Government) and ultimately blocked by Rome; hurt, a year later he suffered a stroke. He recovered enough to make a two-year temperance tour of America, and he died in 1856, aged sixty-six. Archbishop David Mathew purchased the castle in 1938, by which time it had fallen into disrepair, to 'keep it in the family', even as a spectacular Gothic ruin.

It was to be more than forty years after Father Mathew's death that the Pioneers (the Pioneer Total Abstinence Association of the Sacred Heart), was established in Dublin on 27 Dec 1898 by a County Wexford Jesuit, Fr James Cullen. He devised the 'heroic offering' in which people pledged to abstain from alcohol for life and membership reached half a million in the 1950s. It has declined since then, but people can still be seen proudly wearing the Pioneer lapel pin.

Mathew the Grand National winner was bred by John Westropp of Coolreagh, County Clare in 1838, sired by a horse called *Vestris*, who was by the famous *Whalebone*, and sold to Mr Courtenay. The twenty-eight runners for the 1847 running was the biggest field yet. This was the year the name of the race was changed to the Grand National Handicap Steeplechase.

Apart from *Mathew* there was also a very good chestnut mare entered from Ireland called *Brunette.* She had won her last two races and had to carry 12st 6lbs in the National. *Brunette* was to the Irish in the nineteenth century what *Dawn Run* was in the late twentieth. It was reported a hundred years after *Brunette* that 'none of her sex since has held such a place in the affections of the Irish, and the English, steeplechasing public. She was in the 1840s what *Prince Regent* (a gelding) was in the 1940s.'

She was by *Sir Hercules* out of a mare by *Yeoman* and was bred in County Meath by William Allen of Ginnet's. She won the then famous Kilrue Cup, and was bought by John Preston of Bellinter, Navan, Master of the Bellinter Staghounds, and was usually ridden by 'the celebrated Galway horseman', Allen McDonough. She won many races on both sides of the Irish Sea, but one in particular is pertinent to the 1847 Grand National.

It was a race for the Kilrue Cup in April 1846 over a course between Fairyhouse and

Black Bull. Carrying her customary top weight of 12st 7lbs she beat *St Leger* and *Mathew*; *Mathew* was to win the next year's National with *St Leger*, also representing Ireland, second, and *St Leger* was then to win the French equivalent, the Paris Steeplechase.

For the 1847 National *Mathew*, carrying only 10st 6lbs, was favourite, having excelled in a trial on the Curragh the previous week. He was owned by Mr John Courtenay of Ballyedmond, County Cork, a leading figure of the Irish Turf, trained by J. Murphy at The Cottage stables on the Curragh, and ridden by Denis (Denny) Wynne.

A story about his favouritism has come down through the years. The night before the race, with Liverpool filling up with revellers, punters, swells and swagmen, a lady magician claimed she had 'seen' *Mathew* as the winner. The money poured on, so that on the morning of the race he was 4-1, the next best being the 10-1 of the previous year's runner-up *Culverthorpe*. Then for some strange reason that posterity does not record, just before the start of the race, *Mathew*'s price drifted right out to join *Culverthorpe* on 10-1. *Brunette*'s price 'went for a walk in the market' so that even at 30-1 about the great mare she was 'dead meat' and no-one took the price. *Mathew* was described rather unflatteringly by a correspondent as, 'rather stilty on his hind legs, and said legs are very straight. His colour, a rather mealy brown, gave him a somewhat mean look.'

But the same reporter continued, 'But he carried his head proudly, and had a bold confident look of the eye which is one of the signs of fitness and condition. His action, particularly in walking, was remarkably fine, even grand, and his performance showed that a horse is not to be judged by such little points, as we have spoken of, and which we considered to tell against him.'

As *Brunette*, burdened with 12st 6lbs and now thirteen years old on this, her first attempt at the National, and *Mathew* trailed the rest it seemed as if there had been 'those in the know'; the pair looked out of it. At Becher's second time round *Jerry* took the lead and was still leading as he cleared the last hurdle and *St Leger* challenged. Then, seemingly out of nowhere, Denis Wynne, five times leading rider, brought *Mathew* onto the scene to beat *St Leger* by a length, with *Jerry* one length behind, a result that doubtless brought cheers from the thousands of Irish who had their money on Ireland's first winner. *Brunette* finished seventh. It has been suggested that 'half the population' had backed *Mathew* and that the returning mail boats were scenes of great revelry. There is also a sad connection between the Wynne family and Aintree: fifteen years after *Mathew*'s win, Denny Wynne's son James was to have his first ride in the race on Lord de Freyne's *O'Connell*; earlier that morning James received news that his sister had died in Ireland. The owner tried to stop him riding and said he would get him directly to the port; James, young, exuberant, longing to follow in his father's famous footsteps, declined and rode anyway. Near the end of the first circuit, at one of the smaller fences, one horse fell and brought down two others, including *O'Connell*; one of the loose horses then rolled on the prostrate Wynne and caused such severe internal injuries that he died that night in the Sefton Arms outside the course. His grief-stricken parents in Ireland had lost both a son and a daughter on the same day.

But in 1847, after eight years of trying, *Mathew* and Denis Wynne had given the Irish their first win. The only certainty is that their supporters did not remain abstemious during the many celebrations on both sides of the Irish Sea.

3

EARLY IRISH WINNERS

1850-51 – ABD EL KADER; 1855 – WANDERER; 1868 AND 1871 – THE LAMB; 1879 – THE LIBERATOR; 1880 – EMPRESS

In the early days of steeplechasing many of the horses doubled up in other roles; hunting was the primary one, but others worked the plough, pulled the bus, and probably took the family to church on Sunday!

Abd El Kader, or 'Little Ab' as he became affectionately known, was the progeny of a mare who was a leader of the team that pulled the Shrewsbury coach. On a visit to England in 1827, twelve years before the first Grand National, Henry Osborne of Dardistown Castle, Julianstown, Drogheda, County Louth, was impressed enough with her to buy her for 40 guineas (or, in some reports, £50) and take her home to race and to hunt with the Meath.

Dardistown is a medieval castle with two wings, one built in the seventeenth century and one in the eighteenth, the family seat of the Osborne family. Henry Osborne evidently had both a love of racing and an eye for a prospective good horse; apparently he did not demur at the price. He named the coach mare *English Lass* and proceeded to win a number of races with her, including the Bachelors' Plate at nearby Bellewstown; she also proved to be a good hunter before retiring to stud. It was not until her eighth foal (or ninth, according to different reports) that she bred anything that went on to win. This was a small bay colt that would not grow beyond 15.2 hh at maturity. He became the first dual winner of the Grand National, and was named *Abd El Kader*, (which translates roughly as 'servant of the powerful') presumably after the nineteenth-century Algerian resistance leader of that name. He was by *Ishmael*, probably a thoroughbred, out of *English Lass*.

Abd El Kader was to stamp himself into the Aintree record books, not only as the first dual winner but also, in 1851, as the first sub ten-minute time recorded for the race. *Abd El Kader* was one of those little horses not just with a big heart, but also with springs in his heels; keen to go, determined to win, like a gazelle over his fences and quickly away from them on landing; the sort who could take off with two others, but land running when they were still airborne; taking a decent hold of the bit and still on a tight rein coming to the last. There's no greater feeling in jump racing!

Early in his career he suffered a fall that could have finished him, but it didn't dent his appetite and he won so many races that a crack at Aintree seemed viable.

The breeding of racehorses was often not recorded in these early years and yet *Ab*, although a half-bred, had his full parentage listed.

In 1850 he was set to carry 9st 12lbs and was unconsidered in the betting, in spite of his home reputation. There were thirty-two runners and the previous year's winner, *Peter Simple*, 12st 2lbs, was favourite. The weights went right down to 8st 7lbs (*The Pony*), and once more a few horses had travelled over from Ireland.

Peter Simple collided with *The Oaks* at the first, knocking that one out of it while the favourite recovered sufficiently to be sharing the lead by the end of the first circuit. It was as they approached the second Becher's that *Abd El Kader*, ridden by Chris Green, joined them and put in such a great leap that he gained many lengths and sprinted away, bowling along on the mainly good ground; even the plough wasn't too heavy this year. Only *Knight of the Gwynne*, ridden by *Mathew*'s successful jockey Denis Wynne, was able to challenge, but *Ab* won by a length and still looked fresh. The first four home were all Irish-bred, third being Lord Waterford's *Sir John*, and fourth *Tipperary Boy*.

In 1851, many more took notice of *Abd el Kader*, including, inevitably, the handicapper, though only by six pounds. This was the year of the Great Exhibition in Hyde Park, the year that gold was discovered in Australia and when for the first time a submarine telegraph cable was laid between Dover and Calais. It was to be 1994 before the Channel Tunnel, long anticipated, finally came to fruition. It had first been suggested by Napoleon in 1802.

Abd El Kader was now owned by Henry Osborne's son, Joseph, who was the compiler of the Steeple Chase Calendar and Hurdle Race Epitome, published in Dublin in 1849.

He carried 10st 4lbs and was joint second favourite with *Sir John*, behind *Rat-Trap* who had also run the previous year but had collided with another horse. *Sir John* was top weight on 11st 12lbs and this time twenty-one went to post, eleven fewer than the year before. A mare called *Maria Day*, eighth the previous year, carried one pound more than *Ab* and she set about trying to become the first mare to win the race.

It proved a thriller, one that must have been great to watch, and again the weather was clear enabling good viewing.

And again, little *Abd El Kader* made mincemeat of the mighty fences, skipping along merrily towards the rear, behind *Sir John* who led, with a bunch of horses behind him. The favourite, *Rat-Trap*, cried enough, however, refusing a post and rails after a stretch of plough although his rider, the great Jem Mason, managed to get him over it and finished. At the end of the first circuit *Sir John* was still giving his supporters plenty of cause for hope. A number fell but *Ab*, this year ridden by Thomas Abbott, steered clear of trouble and once more put in a smooth forward move. *Maria Day*, ridden by John 'Richard' Frisby, moved closer, too, and as the horses turned for home there were four with a chance; but *Sir John* and *Tipperary Boy* could not go the pace of the little horse and the mare and it was these two who duelled their way up the straight.

It was one of the first epics of the race, up that gruelling long run-in; one can imagine the roar of the crowds, the urging of the jockeys, the cheers for little *Ab* when he prevailed; the verdict given was a neck. *Sir John* again finished third.

Abd El Kader returned to the celebratory bonfires in County Louth.

Both hero and heroine tried again in 1852. Could *Ab* win three years in succession? He had been put up a full stone in the weights. Or could *Maria* become the first mare to win? That accolade went instead to *Miss Mowbray*; *Ab* was pulled up and *Maria* fell. In 1853 *Abd El Kader* tried again and finished fifth. He also ran in the 1858 Grand National as a sixteen-year-old, but uncharacteristically fell at the second fence.

◆ ◆ ◆

Two Irish horses travelled over for the 1855 Grand National, *Boundaway* and *Wanderer*, but their chances were dismissed in cursory fashion by *Bell's Life*. Of *Boundaway*, their correspondent likened him to 'a gawky, narrow clothes' horse', and *Wanderer*'s prospects were disregarded even more damningly: 'a rough, undersized, common-looking hunter'. There cannot be many Grand National winners to have been thus described; Mr John Hanlon, *Wanderer*'s rider, had backed *Boundaway* and *Wanderer* may have been intended as his pacemaker.

Snow or frost caused the race to be postponed, and with the thaw came heavy, gluey ground, which evidently suited *Wanderer*. The lovely mare *Miss Mowbray*, winner in 1852 and runner up the following year, had missed the 1854 race through treachery, having been 'got at'. Not by doping, but by someone administering a 'blister' on the eve of the race when she was already at Aintree, which produced severe inflammation and swelling, leaving her unable to run.

There was at this time still no governing body for steeplechasing – the National Hunt Committee was eventually formed in 1866 – and the Turf Club, far from helping, still looked down its collective nose at its offshoot. There was no liaison between meetings so even if stewards did ban a rider, owner, trainer or anyone else involved with foul play of whatever nature it could only apply to that meeting. It meant *Miss Mowbray*'s connections had had little hope of redress against the perpetrator of the crime to their mare.

A worse fate awaited the mare that had once been dismissed in Newmarket as 'not worth training'. She was not considered robust enough for steeplechasing, but a spell in the hunting field had proved she possessed talent when faced with fences, and she won the National at her first attempt. Sadly, this time she was to take a crashing fall at Becher's Brook, apparently breaking both her neck and back, and was quickly put down.

The race is also remembered for it being the retirement one of Tom Olliver, riding for the seventeenth consecutive time since the inception of the race. He won on *Gay Lad* in 1842, *Vanguard* in 1843 and *Peter Simple* in 1853, and was also second three times: in the inaugural running on *Seventy Four* behind *Lottery*, on *St Leger* behind *Mathew*, and with *The Curate* (to *Chandler*) in 1848; and he was third on *Prince George* (1849). Tom Olliver was to become mentor to Aintree's most successful jockey, George Stevens, who rode his first of five Grand National winners the year following Tom's retirement on *Freetrader* in 1856.

Back to 1855, and Denis Wynne, successful on *Mathew*, was aboard *Little Charley*, an Aintree regular who eventually won in 1858 ridden by William Archer, whose flat racing prodigy son, Fred, was then one year old. Tom Olliver's last mount was Mr Roberts' *Bastion*, and the favourite was the Cheltenham Chase winner, *Trout*. *Miss Mowbray* was top weight on 11.6 and second favourite, followed by *Peter* on 11.4 and *Needwood* on 11.2, but the majority were in the 9 to 10 stone bracket illustrating that this was not, on paper, a National of the best calibre.

The rain was falling as they set off with *Trout* 'swimming' along at the head of affairs as far as Becher's Brook. Near the end of the first circuit *Bastion* joined *Trout* leaping over the water and *Wanderer* was close behind, and he took over the lead when *Trout* slipped. *Freetrader*, too, was moving well and *Miss Mowbray* came into a challenging position only to crash out fatally at Becher's. *Wanderer*'s jockey, John Hanlon, knowing that his money was on *Boundaway*, took a pull, the restraint letting *Trout* and *Freetrader* go by. But *Boundaway* was fading so Hanlon, realising he would not be winning money on *Boundaway*, went for the greater glory of riding the winner; he let out a bit of rein on *Wanderer*, allowing him to regain the lead, and galloped on to victory.

Wanderer, by *Verulam*, was a full horse (not castrated), owned and trained by John Dennis and bred, according to one record, by Mr Holmes in Ireland; the Londsdale Library book *Steeplechasing* has *Verulam* as being sired by the first Grand National winner, *Lottery*, out of *Wire*, a sister to *Whalebone* and *Whisker*, by *Waxy*. *Wire*, foaled in 1811, was brought to Ireland by Lord Sligo and many of the old Irish thoroughbred families go back to her, Charles Richardson's British Steeplechasing regards *Wanderer*'s Grand National as of poor quality, with the first three home on low weights at long prices; the winner was 25-1. The fifth horse, *Dangerous*, had been a bus horse in Cheshire not very long before.

Other books have it that *Wanderer* was a descendent of the unbeaten *Eclipse*. There is an expression '*Eclipse* first, the rest nowhere', and sometimes that was literally the case as half of his eighteen victories were walk-overs; such was his superiority that often no rivals were willing to take him on. That he was truly a great horse was proved beyond doubt, however, at stud: he sired three of the first five Derby winners and has been responsible for numerous direct descendents since then.

◆◆◆

Small, frail and gentle, *The Lamb* was never expected to make a racehorse, let alone become a dual Grand National winner.

A grey horse is always popular with the public and *The Lamb* was possibly the first of that colour to earn his place in their hearts. Surprisingly, only two grey horses have ever won the Grand National, *The Lamb* twice, and *Nicolaus Silver* in 1961. Other greys to have gone close include *Suny Bay*, twice second, in 1997-8; in 2002 *What's Up Boys* was second; and in 2008 *King Johns Castle* was also runner-up. The first of two horses called *Peter Simple* was second in 1845 and third in 1841 and 1842; *Cigar*, also grey, was second in 1841.

The Lamb was bred by a County Clare farmer, Mr Henchy, and had interesting Grand National connections: he was by *Zouave* who had been bred by Mr Courtenay, owner of 1947 winner *Mathew*, and he was out of a mare by *Arthur*, who finished second to *Jerry* in the second Grand National in 1840.

It was Mr Henchy's son, himself delicate and all too soon to die, who christened the gentle youngster *The Lamb*. By the time he was broken in, he stood only 14.3 hh, and although he grew a bit, he was almost certainly the smallest National winner. Before that, he was offered for sale to Edward Studd, owner of the 1866 winner *Salamander*, who had had to overcome deep snow on his way to victory.

Mr Studd's reaction on seeing the tiny *The Lamb* is said to have been,

'He's not fit to carry a man's boots.'

The sale did not take place.

Instead, any thoughts of the little fellow becoming a racehorse were put aside when he was bought by a Dublin veterinary surgeon, Joe Doyle, for £30 for his sickly daughter. She

suffered from consumption, and the idea was that being out in the fresh air on a pony would be good for her. But nevertheless *The Lamb* was a thoroughbred, and almost certainly too 'sharp' for her; for one thing, he often used to jump out of his paddock. Perhaps he should be tried as a racehorse after all? He won a few small races on the flat, and at some stage, either before or after winning the Kildare Hunt Plate at Punchestown, he was leased to Lord Poulett, in whose colours of red jacket and blue sleeves and cap he then ran.

Small enough to contend pony races, he was described thus:

'The slope of his shoulders was as a sculptor's expression of power as they smoothened to the saddle, and his short back swelled to the great galloping power of his quarters and his bony, athletic legs, while the charm that he had held for a delicate boy remained in the grace and beauty of his head and the quiet eye.' – *Grand National 1945* by Con O'Leary

He was now aimed for the 1868 Grand National, a year that saw challengers from France and Germany as well as Ireland. There was a strong wind and the ground was heavy. George Ede, alias Mr Edwards, rode the dark, almost black, grey, who was trained for Lord Poulett by Ben Land senior. The favourite was *Chimney Sweep*; another horse, *Fan*, repeatedly refused the second fence. Every time they encountered the plough *The Lamb* dropped back among the twenty-one runners, but on turf, and with a fence in front of him, he skipped along, avoiding fallen horses all over the place; at one point, being harried by loose horses on either side, his jockey calmly leant over with his whip, first one way and then the other, knocking the offenders out of the way.

Going to the last fence, the race lay between the 'little fella' and the fancied *Pearl Diver*, but it was *The Lamb* who sprinted clear on the run in to score by two lengths.

The Lamb did not run in 1869 due to a clerical error, and missed 1870, suffering from a wasting disease. That he was nursed back to health and returned to win the 1871 National was a credit to all his connections. In the intervening two years George Stevens had won both Nationals on *The Colonel*.

Three months before the 1871 race Lord Poulett had a vivid dream about *The Lamb* winning, seeing clearly not only his colours, but also the face of a particular jockey, Tommy Pickernell, alias Mr Thomas; so he at once secured his services, with the request not to reveal his dream.

The Colonel was bidding for a three timer, but was set to carry 12st 8lb. *Pearl Diver* was again in the line up and so was *Despatch*, owned by Edward Studd who had originally been so disparaging about *The Lamb*'s prospects.

On a day of bright sunshine and perfect going the twenty-five runners set off at a cracking pace, and *The Lamb* was 'pinging' his fences, jumping superbly. At one point, he actually jumped cleanly over two fallen horses as well as the fence itself. At the last fence the race lay between the grey and *Despatch* and, presumably to Edward Studd's chagrin, it was *The Lamb* who once again sprinted clear for another two-length winning margin.

The Colonel finished sixth; three months later his rider, George Stevens, who still holds the Grand National record of five winning rides, was dead, following a fall from his cob on Cleeve Hill, overlooking Cheltenham racecourse.

Before the next year *The Lamb* had been sold to Baron Oppenheim for £1,200 (a contrast to his original purchase sum of £30), and he ran again in the National, but 12st 7lb was just too much for the brave little horse to carry and he finished fourth. He then went to Germany with his new owner and ran in the Grosser Preis von Baden-Baden, ridden by Count Nicholas Esterhazy. With three miles and with all sixteen fences behind them they were winning easily when, a hundred yards before the winning post, he hit a soft patch of ground, broke a leg, and had to be put down, a tragic end to one of the best and bravest fencers – as well as smallest – ever to have conquered Liverpool.

Ninety years separated the two grey winners of the Grand National, but by coincidence, the owners of each were related by marriage; in a sadder coincidence, both horses broke a leg and had to be put down. Bred by James Heffernan in County Tipperary, *Nicolaus Silver* was originally owned and trained by Dan Kirwan near Gowran Park, County Kilkenny; the horse moved to England where Fred Rimell trained him for owner Jeremy Vaughan to win the 1961 race. In the saddle was Bobby Beasley, grandson of Harry, who won the 1891 National on *Come Away*. Bobby Beasley died on January 9, 2008, aged seventy-two.

Although unrelated, *Nicolaus Silver* was, like *The Lamb*, exceptionally good-looking, and he quickly adapted to the Aintree fences. In later years he retired to go hunting in Sussex where, sadly, he broke a leg in a gateway.

◆ ◆ ◆

One thinks of the Curragh as a flat racing centre, the 'Newmarket' of Ireland with its expanse of heath for training and its 'headquarters' racecourse of The Curragh, home to all five Irish Classics and currently undergoing major renovation to put it on a par with the world's top flat racecourses.

Driving by the course is to stir the imagination of great Classic triumphs; but look again, and there beyond the course are also a number of schooling fences. Not only are several of the yards around the Curragh mixed (housing both flat and jumping horses), but also some of them have produced Grand National winners and jockeys.

Tom Ferguson, who had three runners in the very first National, trained from Rossmore Lodge on the Curragh. By all accounts he wasn't the easiest person to live with or work for, but he knew how to produce and train a racehorse. His famous *Harkaway* won eighteen races at the Curragh and beat the best including *Birdcatcher*. Larry Byrne, who rode *Barkston* for Ferguson in the first National, trained from here for a while.

Denny Wynne, winning rider of *Mathew* and five times Irish champion jockey subsequently occupied Rossmore Lodge. His son Joe, who died at Aintree, was twice leading jockey, and another son, Frank, was champion jockey four times before he, in his turn, took over Rossmore Lodge.

Allen McDonough, originally from County Galway, trained from Athgarvan Lodge on the eastern side of the Curragh. His was a 'nearly' story in the Grand National, although he did win the immediate forerunner of the National, riding his own chestnut *Sir William* in the three-runner 1838 race worth just £55, and had been second of four on *Disowned* in 1837. The re-vamped 'first' Grand National of 1839 was worth £590, and then as now prize-money was partly what made it into the most coveted steeplechase; that and the challenge of conquering the most demanding steeple-chase course in the world.

He was seventh in what is generally known as the first Grand National in 1839 on *The Nun*, when his brother, William, was waylaid by a mob on *Rust*. Allen also finished second on *Arthur*, 1840, and *Cigar* in 1841 when his brother William fell with *Legacy*. William suffered bad luck again in 1846 when he was knocked off his horse by a presumably over-exuberant mounted spectator. Both brothers rode, without placing, in 1844, '46, and '47, and William also rode in 1842 and Allen in 1843, again without success.

Once Allen turned to training he still rode a bit, but under an assumed name as was the custom of the day, in his case Captain Williams, although he did not ride in the National again.

Allen McDonough was a top amateur rider and a good trainer, but somewhat feckless with money, gambling so much of it away that he had to sell his best horse, *Trickstress*, shortly before she won the 1872 Irish Derby. Later the same year he sold up and retired to Dublin, from where he still occasionally went hunting. He died in 1888, at the age of eighty-four.

Perhaps the best thing he did as a trainer was to become riding mentor to Tommy Beasley, passing on to the eldest Beasley brother many of his skills in the racing saddle.

In the 1970s Strawhall became the training base of Grand National winning jockey, Eddie Harty, the 1969 victor on *Highland Wedding*; Dermot Weld's Rosewell House, home to many Classic and flat winners worldwide, stabled *Greasepaint* who then finished runner up for a second time in the 1984 Grand National having been bought by Michael Smurfit. Most recently, Frances Crowley, wife of leading Irish flat jockey Pat Smullen, sent out *Nil Desperandum* from Clifton Lodge to finish fourth in the 2006 National.

Conyngham Lodge has a much older Grand National connection, for Algy Anthony, winning rider of *Ambush II* in 1900, trained from here, and before that it was the base for Captain J. F. 'The Shaver' Lee-Barber who dashed his *Jupiter Tonans* into a furlong lead in the 1880 National. Algy Anthony additionally took over another Curragh lodge, Westenra, where he, built a schooling steeplechase course.

Coburg Lodge, latterly also known as Brownstown Lodge, was home of the Maher family whose mare, *Frigate*, was an Aintree specialist and thoroughly deserved her win in 1889.

Ballysax Manor is where *L'Escargot* was trained to win the 1975 National and his 'lad' Mick Ennis moved to Brownstown Lodge until it was demolished. Brownstown House was also the last home to Tommy Beasley.

Eyrefield Lodge is a haven of peace and tranquillity on the eastern edge of the Curragh. Approached along a winding avenue, mares and foals graze in the paddocks in front of the house and stables. The whole is very little altered in two hundred years in which time it has been in the hands of only two families, Linde and Loder. Today, what were the lads' dormitories above a block of stables lie empty, and the private steeplechase course on the farm is long since gone. It is said that every type of fence was replicated and that when the gong sounded for feeding time, the horses turned out in the schooling field had to jump their way back to the yard if they were to be fed! The stables remain barely altered bar the occasional lick of paint: cobblestone floors, high wooden doors with grills, an internal passageway running the length and breadth of them, so that even all that time ago lads did not get too wet in bad weather.

For the last century it has been a top flat racing stud – *Pretty Polly*, winner of twenty-two of her twenty-four races, was bred here and the thirteenth generation of her line continue to pass on her blue blood under the care of Sir Edmund and Lady Loder, her current winner being *Bee Eater*. Originally Eyrefield Lodge was famous for steeple-chasing in general and the Grand National in particular. *Ambush II* was trained here and twenty years before him it housed *Empress* and *Woodbrook* who won the National in 1880 and 1881.

Eyrefield Lodge, like its neighbour Eyrefield House, was built in the 1760s by Linde's grandfather; both were burnt down in 1798, and rebuilt.

Harry Eyre Linde, a sergeant in the Royal Irish Constabulary, but best remembered as an outstanding, clever trainer, came within a whisker of training three Grand National winners in successive years. He succeeded with *Empress* and *Woodbrook*, but had to watch in wonderment as his previous charge, *Seaman*, with a history of unsoundness, galloped to a short-head victory over one of his, *Cyrus*. *Seaman* was ridden by his owner, Lord Manners and it was his first ride, not only in the National, but in any race. Certainly he had the last laugh in his acquisition, whether or not he knew before the race that the pundits had been laughing at him for paying £2,000 for an unsound horse. Interestingly, the under-bidder for Eyrefield Lodge, Richard Dawson, uprooted to England and took with him *Drogheda*, who won the 1898 National the very next year; he was also to train three Derby winners.

It was from Eyrefield House, a little further on from Eyrefield Lodge, that three of the Beasley brothers trained. The five sons of Joseph Laphorn Beasley of Salisbury House, Kildare, Thomas, John (Jack), Harry, James (Jimmy) and Willie enjoyed hunting with an uncle's harrier pack until racing took over. And how. They were the Carberrys of their day. There was at least one of the brothers riding in the Grand National over sixteen consecutive years; James was the only one who never rode in it, being abroad most of the time, but in 1879 the other four all lined up.

Another Curragh lodge to produce a Grand National winning combination was Jockey Hall, home of Garrett Moore and the 1879 hero, the aptly named *The Liberator*, first of a then-unprecedented three Irish-trained winners in a row.

Garrett and his brother Willie (William Henry) grew up under the tuition of their cantankerous father, John Hubert Moore, one of the first trainers to specialise in steeple-chasing. Like Linde at Eyrefield Lodge, he built a steeplechase course on his property and here Garrett, known as Gary, learnt much of what it takes to be a jump jockey, putting the tuition he received to good effect. With *Scots Grey* he won the Irish Grand Nationals

of 1872 and 1875, and finished eighth in the 1872 Grand National, and with *The Liberator* he won the 1875 Galway Plate; Garrett gained further Aintree experience when riding *Pride of Kildare* into third place in the 1878 National, one year before his victory on *The Liberator* whose third attempt at the race it was. *The Liberator* had fallen in 1876 for another owner and jockey and finished third in 1877, ridden for Garrett Moore by 'Mr Thomas', alias Tommy Pickernell who won the National three times.

The Liberator was by *Daniel O'Connell* out of a mare called *Mary O'Toole*. Daniel O'Connell, the man, (1775-1847) was known as The Liberator, chiefly for his work for the emancipation of Catholics. A Kerryman from Derrynane, near Waterville, he was a barrister who became increasingly involved with politics. He was a founder of the Catholic Association and by opening it to anyone who could pay a subscription of one penny a month it soon became a voice of and for the masses. He earned the admiration of millions in his aim to repeal the Act of the Union.

The horse *The Liberator* first ran in the Grand National in 1876 when he fell. He was subsequently sent to the sales but failed to sell at auction; outside the ring he was bought by Garrett Moore for £500.

Gary was determined to win the National on the bay gelding, but shortly before his 1879 attempt the horse came home lame from a gallop; luckily it was not a lasting injury

and the now ten-year-old lined up alongside seventeen others, exactly half of them ridden by amateurs. It was an era of small fields and Corinthian riders, but nevertheless there was no such thing as an easy Grand National, and in fact there was every prospect of a close contest as all the runners, unusually, were weighted within 22lbs of each other; the 1876 winner *Regal*, the favourite, was on top weight of 11st 10lb, and the bottom weight was *Concha* on 10st 2lb.

Tom Beasley settled *Martha*, a rank outsider at 50-1, into a handy position and she ran a cracking race, only conceding to the winner and second, *Jackal*, at the last obstacle. *Jackal* was first to challenge, but Garrett Moore had ridden a patient race; all he had to do now was let the reins out a notch on *The Liberator* and fly by for a ten-length victory.

Three of the four Beasley brothers completed the course; besides Tommy's third on *Martha*, Willie finished eighth on *Lord Marcus* and Harry was ninth on *Turco*; *Victor II* and Harry pulled up.

Harry's turn was to come.

The Empress Elizabeth of Austria, wife of Emperor Franz Josef, and her sister, the Queen of Naples, used to make incognito visits to Ireland mainly for the hunting in Meath where

INSPECTING THE BLACK
6ft 3 DROP (12ft if you drop in the ditch)
AT BECHER'S

they cut a fine dash,
but also for the steeple-
chasing. As children they had
learnt to jump without stirrups and
their appearances enlivened an already
exciting hunting and steeple-chasing scene; they were
admired wherever they went.

The Empress used to arrive by train from Dublin to Maynooth, and from there she was
conveyed by horse and carriage to Summerhill House, County Meath. One day when out
hunting the stag jumped over the wall into the grounds of Maynooth College, the seminary;
unfazed, the Empress alone followed.

Elizabeth was a regular visitor to Eyrefield Lodge, and it was in her honour that *Empress* was named. Also at Eyrefield, one day the Empress admired a two-year-old jumping fault-lessly twice round the private steeplechase course, and exclaimed that it was 'too good'. Subsequently named *Too Good*, the horse won the Grande Steeplechase de Paris of 1883 and finished second in the 1886 Grand National to *Old Joe*.

Empress was a chestnut mare by *Blood Royal* out of *Jeu des Mots*, bred by Thomas Lindesay. As a three-year-old she ran on the flat without success in Harry Eyre-Linde's colours, but once she was jumping she won five of her seven races.

Empress lived up to expectations so well that shortly before the 1880 National a Mr. P. Ducrot bought her. It quite often happens that an intended National runner changes hands shortly before the race; it can be that the new owner simply wants the pleasure of owning a runner, but it is more likely to be the purchase of a horse with a decent chance – if the would-be buyer's pocket is long enough and if the vendor is willing to sell. King Edward VII did it with *Moifaa* and it still happens today.

Linde retained the training of *Empress* and Tommy Beasley kept the ride. A golden chest-nut, her coat glistened in the sunshine on March 19, 1880, when she lined up with thirteen others for the big race. She was only five years old, but was a strong type with good shoulders and a short back, just the sort to jump well and with agility; any horse trained by Harry Eyre-Linde was going to be well-versed in jumping, and well-backed.

Even for a race with such a small field, it was remarkable that only two falls were recorded, while two more horses refused. *The Liberator* the reigning Grand National trophy-holder was allocated 12st 7lb, three horses were on 11.11, one, *Woodbrook*, was on 11.7, and the remainder ranged from 10st 7lb to 10st 2lb. *Regal*, sixth behind *The Liberator* the previous year, was favourite, the holder was joint second favourite with *Wild Monarch*, followed by a grey, *Downpatrick* then *Empress* on 8-1. *Jupiter Tonas* was one of three on 50-1 and *Dainty* was on 66-1. *Shifnal*, winner two years before, was un-fancied at 20-1.

Soon they were off and at the second fence *Regal*, the favourite, fell. *Downpatrick* led them along until 'Shaver' Lee-Barber took *Jupiter Tonans* into the lead; at the end of the first circuit he was rejoined by the grey, but then 'Shaver' shot his horse into such a long lead that he was soon a furlong ahead. It seemed impossible for him to retain that pace and position, for all that he was a previous Irish National winner. Some way behind him Tommy Beasley had been nearly knocked out of *Empress*'s saddle and lost a stirrup iron; it took him awhile to regain it but he knew there was still a long way to go. Gradually, steadily, he made up the lost ground; last year's victor *The Liberator* was moving forward, too, and the pair wore down the leader at about the second last. A great duel looked in prospect, but the mare was receiving two stone in weight from *The Liberator* and it was too much for him. Approaching the last fence, *Empress* was said to put in a leap nearly as prodigious as *Lottery*'s way back in 1839, and that settled the issue; she ran out a two-length winner. She was the fourth five-year-old to win, and there has been only one since, the French challenger *Lutteur* in 1909. In 1931 the minimum age was set at six, and since 1987 it has been seven.

Among the spectators that day was the Prince of Wales; the following year the Empress of Austria herself was among the visitors in bitter, snowy conditions, but *Empress* the mare never ran again. She was retired to stud where her most successful descendant was *Red Prince II* who won the 1893 Lancashire Steeplechase.

The next year was again to be a Linde-Beasley combination.

4

THE BEASLEY CONNECTION

1881 – WOODBROOK; 1889 – FRIGATE;
1891 COME AWAY

TOMMY AND HARRY BEASLEY were the best-known of the famous Beasley brothers.

Tommy was as good a flat race jockey as he was over fences, and rode three Irish Derby winners, in 1887 *Pet Fox*, 1889 *Tragedy* and 1891 *Narraghmore*. His Grand National record was excellent, three wins, two seconds and a third from twelve rides, with only two falls. He also lodged one of only two objections in the history of the race when *Shifnal* beat him into second place on *Martha* in 1878. He accused jockey John Jones, on the winner, of foul riding but the objection was overruled. He was also involved in one of only three head finishes – in which he lost to *Seaman*; the others to win by a head were *Alcibiade* (1865), and *Battleship* (1938).

In 1881, fresh from his victory on *Empress* the previous year, Tommy lined up with *Woodbrook*. The conditions were very different; this time instead of a fine clear day it was

THE BEASLEY BROTHERS' AINTREE RECORD

1877	Sultana	Tommy	5th
1878	Martha	Tommy	2nd (to **Shifnal**)
1879	Martha	Tommy	3rd
1879	Lord Marcus	Willie	8th
1879	Turco	Harry	10th
1879	Victor II	Jack	pulled up
1880	Empress	Tommy	WON
1880	Woodbrook	Harry	5th
1880	Victoria	Jack	8
1881	Woodbrook	Tommy	WON
1881	Fairwind	Harry	fell
1882	Cyrus	Tommy	2nd (to **Seaman**)
1882	Mohican	Harry	fell
1883	Zitella	Tommy	5th
1883	Mohican	Harry	fell
1884	Frigate	Harry	2nd (to **Voluptuary**)
1884	Zitella	Tommy	5th
1884	Satellite	Jack	pulled up
1885	Frigate	Harry	2nd (to **Roquefort**)
1886	Too Good	Harry	2nd (to **Old Joe**)
1886	Lady Tempest	Willie	8th
1887	Too Good	Harry	pulled up
1887	Spahi	Tommy	fell
1887	The Hunter	Willie	fell
1888	Frigate	Willie	2nd (to **Playfair**)
1888	Usna	Harry	pulled up
1889	Frigate	Tommy	WON
1889	The Fawn	Willie	7th
1889	Battle Royal	Harry	9th
1890	Frigate	Tommy	brought down
1891	Come Away	Harry	WON
1891	Cruiser	Tommy	5th
1892	Flying Column	Willie	5th
1892	Billee Taylor	Harry	ran out

a mix of rain and snow, and the going was atrocious. All the same, the Empress of Austria braved the elements to watch the race won the previous year by the mare named in her honour.

Woodbrook was a seven-year-old chestnut owned and bred by Captain T.Y.L. Kirkwood, who named him after his home. Also racing were *The Liberator*, carrying 12st 7lb and *Regal II*, carrying 12 stone.

At first glance, *Woodbrook*'s appearance, showing him as scrawny, thin and poor looking, is to beggar belief that he was the sort of horse who could gallop through the atrocious going – plough and mangold field included – yet that is precisely what he did. As all around him floundered, he galloped on as if it were perfect ground.

Any horse from the Eyre academy was bound to garner support, and so it was no surprise that *Woodbrook* started favourite; after all, quite apart from the trainer, the jockey was on a roll, for Tommy Beasley's record in the last three Nationals was second, third and first. It was to continue first, second, fifth.

It was perhaps a surprise to see *The Liberator*, now twelve years old, cutting out most of the running on the first circuit until uncharacteristically falling at the fence after Valentines. Garrett Moore remounted him and they completed the rest of the course to finish last.

Meanwhile *The Liberator*'s fall left *Woodbrook* in the lead and from there on every time a horse tried to challenge him he simply galloped on leaving his rivals toiling in the mire.

There were surely jubilant scenes as, for the third successive year, the Grand National trophy went back to Ireland.

After such fantastic wins in 1880 and 1881, Tommy Beasley could be forgiven for expecting to make it a hat trick in 1882.

There were twelve starters; yet again *The Liberator*, thirteen years old, was handicapped on 12.7, reminiscent of *Lottery* in the past, and similar to what was to happen to *Manifesto* in the next decade. (*Manifesto* won with 12st 7lb in 1899 and carried an incredible 12st 13lb into fourth place in 1900 and 12st 8lb into an astonishing third place at the age of fourteen. Even at an unprecedented sixteen years old he carried 12st 1lb to be last of eight finishers, ridden by Ernie Piggott, grandfather of Lester.)

No horse has been asked to carry 12st 7lb since *Freebooter* in 1952 when the 1950 winner fell. *Mont Tremblant*, *Royal Tan*, and *Early Mist* carried 12st 5lb, 12st 4lb and 12st 2lb respectively in the 1950s, since when the top weight has never been more than 12 stone, and the last horse to carry that weight was *Young Kenny*, who fell at the tenth fence in 2000, but in the 1970s *Red Rum* was top weight in the last four of his five runs, winning under 12 stone in 1974, and second the following year with the same weight. When he won for the third time his weight was 11st 8lb.

At the 1881 National, the course was white with snow as the runners were sent on their way, with *Eau de Vie* romping along in the lead until a broken stirrup-leather put him out of the race after the second Becher's. The snow was falling down making viewing difficult, but when they came back on to the course it was Tom Beasley on *Cyrus* and his lordship on *Seaman* who were ahead of the next year's winner, the mare *Zoedone*. Poor *Seaman* broke down (tore a tendon) at the last and it looked a Tommy triumph all the way. But in one of the bravest efforts of any horse, and a real feat of horsemanship from an amateur riding in his first ever race, Lord Manners and *Seaman* redoubled their efforts and just got up to win.

As for *Eau de Vie*, his was a real bad luck story, for the very next day he turned out again and won the Sefton Chase, a shorter distance over the same fences, by 15 lengths.

Seaman never ran again but his thoughtful owner retired him to become his hack and his children's pet. History does not record what Linde and Beasley thought of 'the one that got away'.

Harry Eyre Linde died in 1897 and although he married twice he left no issue so Eyrefield Lodge was put up for auction. He was a colossus of Irish racing of his time, but he began in a small way with a £25 mare called *Highland Mary*. She won a race in Fairyhouse in 1873 and produced just one foal, *Eyrefield*. He was tiny, little more than a pony, but got the Linde establishment rolling: in 1881 as a four-year-old he won the Prince of Wales Plate at Punchestown and was sold to Germany for £1,000. In addition to his Grand National training feats, Linde also trained three winners of the Irish Grand National, most of the big Irish steeplechases, and the Grande Steeplechase de Paris twice, with *Whisper Low* and *Too Good*. On the flat he trained an Irish Derby winner, *Pet Fox*, in 1887, and won the National Produce Stakes five years running and the Beresford Stakes three consecutive times. Harry Eyre Linde was also leading owner seven times. It was the good fortune of Eyrefield Lodge that as it came out of Linde hands it passed on to the Loder family

◆ ◆ ◆

The Grand National record of *Frigate* is up there with the best of them. She ran in seven Grand Nationals, (as did *The Liberator*, *Why Not* and three others in the history of the race; only *Manifesto* ran in eight), and she finished second, second, fell, seventh, second, first (at last) and brought down.

Frigate was a well-bred bay mare by *Gunboat* out of *Fair Maid of Kent*. This was breeding that could have seen her running on the flat, but her owner, breeder and trainer Mr Mattias Aiden Maher gave her time to mature, taking her hunting as a four-year-old with the Wexford hounds. Mr Maher had bought the dam from the Whitney family of Rathnure.

Mr Maher hailed from Ballinkeele, Enniscorthy, County Wexford, and was to become, in 1889, Senior Steward of the INHS committee and a Steward of the Irish Turf Club.

When *Frigate*'s racing career began she won Punchestown's coveted Conyngham Cup of 1883 ridden by Harry Beasley, and several more in Ireland before crossing the water to Liverpool. It was Harry who then rode her in her first two attempts at Aintree in 1884-5. As a six-year-old she came up against a horse of even bluer blood, *Voluptuary*, bred by Queen Victoria, and a runner in the 1881 Derby, and this was the horse that produced the faster finishing speed on the run-in.

The next year saw *Frigate* again take the number two berth, (to *Roquefort*, ridden, like *Voluptuary* by Mr E.P. Wilson), after which she was sold to a Mr Broadwood and then a Mr Lawrence; in neither of the next two Nationals did she shine for these two men, but somehow Mr Maher was persuaded to buy her back for £500, and within a week she won a race worth exactly that amount. She resumed her Aintree stride, ridden in 1888 by Willie Beasley, again into second place, to *Playfair*. It might have been a winning story had she not been badly interfered with in the race: another runner, *Usna*, veered off the course and almost into the canal, taking *Frigate* with him; only Willie Beasley's skilful horsemanship got her back into the race. The mishap had cost them fifty lengths; they were beaten ten lengths at the finish, and so must rank as one of the genuine hard luck stories in the history of the race.

For 1889 it was yet another Beasley, the third, to ride her. The weather was fine and the going good as the twenty runners lined up; it was *Frigate*'s sixth attempt and she had been second three times. *Roquefort* was favourite and the Prince of Wales had two runners, *Magic* and *Hettie*. Willie Beasley rode *The Fawn*, Harry rode *Battle Royal* and it was Tommy on *Frigate*. It turned into an excellent race, firstly with a ding-dong between *Why Not* and *The Fawn*; *Roquefort* moved up to challenge, but fell at the last open ditch, while Tommy, a canny Aintree rider, moved *Frigate* ever closer. Approaching the last only *Why Not* was ahead of him. Could the perennial bridesmaid carrying Mr Maher's colours of purple and white sleeves get by him? As she battled past to win by a length her perseverance and tenacity was rewarded with rousing cheers from the stands. For *Why Not* it was the start of a not dissimilar Aintree trail, his seven runs finally culminating with a win on his fifth attempt in 1894.

Twenty minutes after the start of *Frigate*'s successful foray on the great race a telegram arrived in Wexford stating that *Frigate* had won. That night tar-barrels blazed in Enniscorthy and Wexford for, according to *The Free Press* 'it was a regular harvest for the sporting men.'

It was rumoured that Mr Maher had won £3,000 on the mare and a big homecoming was prepared with crowds of people turning out to see her – but instead she was taken quietly home.

The year after *Frigate*'s win, 1890, her three-parts brother, *Kentish Fire*, won the Irish Derby. Of only thirteen mares ever to have won the National, ten were in the nineteenth

century, three in the twentieth and so far none in the twenty-first. In 1891 *Frigate* made her seventh and final appearance, but was brought down by a riderless horse on the second circuit. She was retired to stud, but died three years later, to be buried standing with saddle and bridle.

Tommy Beasley had won three Nationals; two years later, in 1891, it was at last Harry's turn, on *Come Away*. Until then he had ridden in the race eleven times, falling two years in succession in 1881 and 1882, coming third in 1883, followed by three seconds in a row, 1884-6.

Harry Beasley was perhaps the most remarkable of the brothers, certainly for his longevity both in the saddle and in life. He was born in 1852 and so was nearly forty when he finally won the National, an age by which most NH jockeys have hung up their racing boots; but to Harry he was a mere spring chicken for he was to be still racing at twice that age. At seventy-two he was beaten by a head by his own son, Willie, in a 4½-mile steeplechase at Punchestown (and is reported to have booed him); and at an amazing seventy-three years old he won his last steeplechase. Nor was that the end of his career: he rode on the flat for the last time at an astonishing eighty-two years old (not allowed in the modern day).

In his career, in addition to his Grand National efforts, he won the Conyngham Cup six times, and he won the Grande Steeplechase de Paris on *Too Good* in 1883 and on *Royal Meath* in 1890. He also won the Grand Hurdle at Auteuil on *Seaman* and he won the Grand Sefton over the Aintree fences four times, on *Jupiter Tonans*, *Lord Chancellor*, *Zitella* and *St George*.

His very last ride in a race, in 1935, was on board a four-year-old mare named *Mollie* in the Corinthian Plate at Baldoyle. Just four years later he died at home at Eyrefield House, on October 19, 1939, and was buried in Newbridge, the County Kildare town close to the Curragh. Eyrefield House went into the ownership of Prince Aly Khan in order to avoid his father the Aga Khan's main stud, Sheshoon, from having to be ploughed up in compulsory wartime tillage. Prince Aly was also an amateur rider – he won a bumper (National Hunt flat race, designed for future jumpers and not open to regular Flat racehorses) in Kilbeggan, the midlands track that day seeing one of its biggest crowds not only to watch the prince, but more especially to see his girlfriend, Hollywood actress Rita Hayworth. The Aga died in 1957 and his son in a car crash three years later.

Eyrefield House in later years was the birthplace of the great steeplechaser *Mill House*.

Harry Beasley was the only person ever to ride *Come Away*; he also trained him, sometimes in unorthodox fashion, for when there was a cold snap he would take him out in the middle of the night. His reasoning was this: the horse had 'dodgy' legs (probably tendon

trouble), and Harry's idea of galloping him by the light of storm lanterns was so that he could work on the turf before it had been hardened by frost; one suspects it may also have been to keep out of sight of the touts, but that is conjecture.

Come Away was a tall bay with strong hindquarters, a long, narrow neck and fine head. He was well bred, by *Cambuslang* out of *Larkaway*, and by the time he came to the Grand National he had shown his ability with two Conyngham Cups at Punchestown, a Valentine Chase over the Aintree fences, and several other wins under his belt; he had also missed a year through leg trouble.

From the twenty-one runners in the 1891 National, four were past winners: *Ilex*, *Roquefort*, *Gamecock* and *Voluptuary*, and two were future ones, *Why Not* and *Cloister*, in addition to *Come Away* himself.

It proved to be a class National, too, with *Cloister* making much of the early running; he was joined by *Roquefort* and *Gamecock*, but as these two began to falter on the second circuit it was *Come Away* who joined *Cloister*, *Ilex* and *Why Not*. It was not to be *Why Not's* year for he fell at the second last, leaving a tight tussle to develop between *Cloister* and *Come Away*. Gamesmanship and jockey-craft came into play. *Cloister*'s jockey, Captain Roddy Owen, tried to 'squeeze up the inner'; (that is, to challenge between the running rails and the rival, instead of using up more ground by coming out round him to pass; the rails also help keep a horse on a straight line). Harry Beasley, however, prevented the captain from achieving his aim by sticking to his rails position, effectively blocking his rival's passage through.

Come Away battled all the way to the line to score by a length. The Captain lodged one of only two objections in the history of the race, but was over-ruled. *Cloister* was second again the following year when Captain Owen rode the winner, *Father O'Flynn*. The year after that, 1893, was *Cloister*'s turn, by a record forty lengths, this time ridden by Bill Dollery. For *Come Away* it was the end of an illustrious career, for he broke down and never ran again.

Tommy Beasley gave up steeplechasing in 1892 at the age of forty-four after winning Punchestown's Kildare Hunt Cup. He won his last flat race in August 1900, at fifty-two years old, and two days later rode his last race, losing an enthralling duel by a head to his younger brother, Harry who was riding a horse called *Too Good* (not be confused with another horse of the same name of a few years earlier). It was twenty-four years since they had first race-ridden along side each other, and on that occasion Tommy had won easily.

Tommy, Harry and their brothers enhanced the Irish racing scene for more than half a century, and rightly go down in the annals as great Grand National riders.

ASTRIDE THE CENTURIES

1895 – WILD MAN FROM BORNEO;
1900 – AMBUSH II

THE WIDGER FAMILY from Waterford have lived, breathed and dreamed the Aintree Grand National for about 130 years. In the current generation, Jerry Widger has attended the last forty Nationals without a break.

Racing, and especially the Grand National, gets into the blood; for some it is inherited, for others it is something that simply starts the adrenalin pumping, the competitive spirit rising, the dream dreaming.

Back in the late nineteenth-century Joe Widger was the youngest of five brothers so he had to take rough and tumble in his stride, to 'sink or swim'; he swam – and how.

Their father, Thomas, was a well-known and respected horse dealer, and young Joe virtually grew up on a horse. There was always something to ride, to produce, to sell, be it a racehorse, pony or cavalry remount.

A local newspaper article written before the family's Grand National win reveals:

The name of Widger has long been 'familiar as a household word' in 'horsey' and horse-buying circles. The business was founded some thirty years ago by Mr Thomas Widger, who has retired from it for sometime in favour of his five sons, all of whom are now actively engaged in its management. The premises are most complete, and cover about an acre and a half of ground. The buildings include stables, loose boxes, carriage houses, harness rooms, etc.; a large covered paddock for showing horses to intending buyers; offices, etc.; and have ample accommodation in every way, and maintained in the finest order for conducting a large business of this description. The Messrs. Widger executer heavy commissions for the English, Dutch, and Italian Governments and for the nobility and gentry of the United Kingdom, and are large dealers on their own account in various classes of horses, which include hunters, race horses, troopers, carriage horses, hacks, etc. of which upwards of 2,000 pass annually through their hands.

The partners have five farms in the vicinity of about seven hundred acres in all, keep half a dozen highly-bred sires, and from three to four hundred horses. The scene in their yard is frequently a lively one when patrons meet to inspect their stock; and there is usually sufficient attraction in the way of horseflesh to draw racing, hunting and army gentlemen thither. The partners are enthusiastic in all horsey matters, have had several successful racehorses, Mr Thomas Widger, Jun., having reached 4th place in three Grand Nationals [6th 1884, 4th Downpatrick 1883,]; Mr Joseph Widger, being successful in 1891 with Libble Drake at Kempton Park, a few days after at Sandown, and again at Gatwick. This horse is the property of Mr Richard Widger. Sarsfield, winner of the Irish International Steeplechase at Leopardstown this year, is the property of Mr John Widger, born in the summer of 1884, and who is well known through-out the kingdom as 'Jack'. At five years of age this little wonder rode in a drag hunt, over 4½ miles of natural country, without a single mishap; and in 1891, at the Dublin Horse Show, took first prize on three consecutive days against a heavy field of competitors. Again 'Jack' was to the fore in a match at Clonmel, which he won easily, after clearing in grand style a stone fence five feet six inches in height, a task which would cause some uneasiness in the minds of some of our most noted cross-country riders, and no doubt there is a great future before this young jockey, who has the advantage of a thorough training at the hands of his father and uncles. 'Jack' is a great favourite with his grandfather (the origi-nal founder), who devotes most of his well-earned leisure to his farm, where he maintains a fine herd of cattle and a superb flock of sheep. Like him his sons are 'to the manner born,' and, as judges, stand second to none. All are as popular as they are widely known in the circles with which their avocation brings them into contact.

Joe was born in 1864 and at ten years old he won a pony race on the sands at Woodstown, County Waterford. At eleven he won a pukka horse race, riding a mare for his father at Castletown. But then he was sent away to school in Mountrath, County Laois; it was a long way from home. Imagine his parents' reaction when they read in the newspaper that their youngest son had won a race in Bangor, north Wales, having somehow escaped school and taken a ferry to Holyhead. Then at seventeen Joe recorded one of those racing feats that will only seldom face a jockey – and are even more rarely overcome. He was riding a horse called *Tom Jones* in a three-mile chase at Cork Park in June 1881. After a mile the bridle broke. For two miles Joe guided, steered and controlled the horse, and stayed in the saddle with no assistance from the bridle, using his body weight, balancing himself every inch of the way – and won the race by two lengths.

It was as a family that the Widgers set out to find a likely Grand National horse; Joe and his four brothers didn't hurry in their quest, but eventually they decided that they liked the look of *Wild Man From Borneo*. The chestnut gelding, by *Decider* out of *Wild Duck* by *Sheldrake*, had run third in the Conyngham Cup and second to *Father O'Flynn* in a chase at Liverpool, so he was likely to both stay and jump the Aintree fences. Bred in Nenagh, County Tipperary, by Mr George Keays, the Widgers bought *Wild Man* as a five-year-old from his Clonsilla, County Dublin, owner James Maher for £600 (no relation to *Frigate*'s owner).

They all seemed to have a 'leg' in him: he ran in the colours of John Widger from 1894 to 1896, and those of Miss F. E. Norris, the future Mrs Joe Widger, in 1897. Joe Widger rode *Wild Man From Borneo* in 1894 to 1895, and again in 1897, but in 1896 he was ridden by Tom Widger.

The brothers set about their Aintree campaign in earnest; they decided to stable him in England, and set themselves up with trainer James Gatland in the chocolate-box, flint-stone, picturesque village of Alfriston on the South Downs, not all that far from Findon, Brighton and Lewes, Sussex. James Gatland had produced *Father O'Flynn* to win the 1892 race, which may have influenced the brothers' choice. It was not long afterwards that *Wild Man* rewarded them with his first win for the family, winning a £500 race at Nottingham, in December 1893, almost repaying their initial outlay at the first time of asking.

So it was with high hopes that they set off for Aintree the following March. It was a perfect day for the fourteen runners that went to post; *Wild Man* was right out at 40-1 in the betting, but he ran a cracking race. Two fences from home the race lay between the Widgers' horse, the veteran *Why Not* and a mare, *Lady Ellen II*. It was poetic justice that

Why Not, at more than twice the age of the two six-year-old challengers, should win at last; he became one of only two thirteen-year-olds to win the race (the other being *Sergeant Murphy* in 1923). The 1853 winner, *Peter Simple*, was fifteen.

Joe Widger vowed to return, and to win; he had learned a lot from his first Aintree experience, and for the next year he made sure he got himself as fit as the horse. The conditions, though, were as bad as the previous year had been good, not just on race day, but also in the preceding month: the rain came down in torrents making the ground too slippery to work on; he had to be galloped on the sand at low tide at Bournemouth, and was withdrawn from his prep race at Gatwick.

Race day, Friday 29 March 1895, brought heavy ground with 'fog as thick as darkness', in other words, abysmal. But the Waterford supporters travelled over in droves two days before. *Aesop*, second to *Cloister* two years previously, started favourite and *Wild Man From Borneo* was the punters' third choice at 10-1 among the nineteen starters. Unknown to all there, it was also the first appearance of a horse who was to become one of the race legends, *Manifesto*; the seven-year-old by *Man of War* out of *Vae Victis* was ridden for his then owner, Harry Dyas, by Terry Kavanagh. At that time he was owned and trained in Ireland; (when he won in 1897 he was trained by Willie McAuliffe in Everleigh on Salisbury Plain, Wiltshire at The Crown Inn; and by W.H. Moore for his 1899 victory, when the actual licence-holder was John Collins.)

Why Not lined up once more and, incredibly for the current trophy holder, started at 50-1, along with four others; just one, *Caustic* was out on 100-1 (he fell) – not that spectators could see much, for apart from heavy ground for the horses to contend with, there was also thick fog.

Aesop led for much of the first circuit and by the time the runners came into view of

those in the grandstands there were six close together over the water where the second favourite, *Horizon* was brought down. *Aesop* was running a great race, clearing Becher's for the second time still in the lead, followed by *Dalkeith* who blundered there, *Father O'Flynn*, *Cathal* and *Manifesto* all close up. But *Aesop* fell at the Canal Turn leaving *Cathal* in the lead, and now it was *Manifesto*, *Wild Man From Borneo* and *Lady Pat* in close contention.

Cathal tried to make the best of his way home and still led over the last, but this time Joe Widger had the leader well within his sights; riding a peach of a race, he gradually wore him down on that long, long run-in, to score by one and a half lengths from *Cathal*.

Wild Man ran again the following two years, but fell or was knocked over in 1896 and pulled up in '97. His '96 rider was Thomas Widger, while Joe rode the stable's better fancied horse, *Waterford* who was also brought down (or fell). Mr M. Widger's *Miss Baron* ridden by T. Kavanagh also fell; (some reports have it that Michael was riding).

The *Waterford News* commented, 'In Waterford the amount of money lost over Joe

Widger's mount would buy an Atlantic liner. It is positively asserted that a local smith pawned his anvil to back the horse.'

◆ ◆ ◆

Long and many were the celebrations among the Widgers in Waterford after *Wild Man*'s 1895 win, and a hundred years later they happily did so all over again, putting on an anniversary party for some two hundred people in 1995, a good many Widger descendants among them. Also attending was Aintree's long-standing head groundsman and stable manager, Ossie Dale, who had begun his Aintree career as the horse ploughman in 1953.

Ossie was first of all taken on a tour of the National Stud in Kildare, which was donated to the country by its previous owner, Mr William Hall-Walker (later Lord Wavertree) whose *The Soarer* won the 1896 Grand National. Ossie then moved on to the reception in Waterford Town Hall, where the huge 1895 trophy took pride of place on the top table.

The next day it was on to racing in Tramore and the feature Wild Man From Borneo Chase. Ossie had brought with him an Aintree flag that proudly flew from Tramore's flagpole for the day.

Ossie Dale has more reason than most, bar the Widgers, to recall *Wild Man From Borneo*. He was out mowing the course one day and had just drawn level with Becher's Brook when his eye caught what looked like a horse's head in the brook. It *was* a horse's head. The stuffed head of *Wild Man*, no less, that had been stolen some time before. Apparently the head had been presented to the Tophams in the spring of 1942, at the time when Liverpool was being blitzed; the racecourse was taken over by the War Office, the land being used to train cadets to ride, and the stands as a staging post for the wounded on their way to hospital.

After Ossie found the head it was mounted in the old weighing room part of the museum, where it hung for a few years. Later it was moved to the Freebooter room (where the winning connections are wined and dined) in case it 'scared children on visits to the Museum' – although it could be that many children enjoy that sort of thing! But in any case,

its condition deteriorated and it is believed that it is now stored in a shed on the course.

The Widgers' Aintree connection did not end with *Wild Man*. In 1903 they ran *Matthew*, who fell; and in 1904 their *The Gunner* finished third behind *Moifaa*.

◆ ◆ ◆

When Lord Marcus Beresford visited the Curragh stables of 'Tommy' Lushington to ask him to look out for a suitable Grand National horse for the Prince of Wales, Lushington, who had ridden for the Prince in England, replied,

'I have the very horse here.'

This was a bold statement, for the horse in question had failed to reach his reserve price of just 50 guineas at auction at two years old, and in addition the un-raced now four-year-old had 'curby' hocks; that is to say, the equivalent of the knees on the hind legs had bony growths known as a curbs; this can cause lameness, or at least be a weakness.

But Lushington had a good eye for a horse as well as being one of the best amateur riders and respected trainers of his time. He had paid £400 for the former cast-off to his breeder William Ashe of Narraghmore and now sold him to the Prince for a not unreasonable £500. More to the point, he retained the training of the brown gelding by *Ben Battle* (also the grandsire of *Manifesto*) who was named *Ambush II*.

Grattan Wildman Lushington (1860-1917), known affectionately to all, including the stable lads, as Mr Tommy, was born in Kent and educated at Cheltenham where he excelled in real tennis, lawn tennis and cricket. It was while serving with the 2nd Queen's Royal West Surrey Regiment that he first visited Ireland, and fell in love with its racing. He was stationed in Cork where he met Noble Johnson with whom he was later to train, first at Conygham Lodge and then Eyre Lodge, both on The Curragh; Ireland became his adopted country. Firstly, after resigning his commission, he joined the stables of T.G. Gordon at Brownstown on The Curragh, and then Jockey Hall. One of the horses

stabled there was *Tragedy* who won the Irish Derby in 1889, and sired a St Leger winner.

Lushington entered the race-riding world with the fervour of a keen young man, and travelled far and wide to ride whatever he could. His first ride was on a mare of his own called *Alda* at the United Hunts Club meeting at Lisgoold, County Cork, and he notched his first win at Roscommon on a horse called *Newgrove* in 1887. Possibly the best chaser he rode was *Battle Royal* on whom he won a Grand Sefton Chase over the Aintree fences; so it was with a good deal of hope that he rode the horse in the 1890 Grand National itself, under the pseudonym Thomas Wildman, but the pair fell at the seventh (the fence after Becher's), remounted and pulled up at the twenty-second; the previous year the horse had been ridden into ninth place by Harry Beasley.

At about this time, after the death of Mr Henry Eyre Linde, Lushington was asked by Major Eustace Loder to purchase Eyre Lodge for him, giving him a limit of £6,000. Lushington bravely bid to £8,000, a boldness that reaped handsome rewards. Eyre Lodge had already housed Grand National winners *Empress*, 1880, and *Woodbrook*, 1881; now it was to become the birthplace of perhaps the greatest flat race filly of all time, *Pretty Polly*, and to house another Grand National winner, *Ambush II*.

Pretty Polly won twenty-two of her twenty-four races in a career spanning four years, including the fillies' Triple Crown of 1,000 Guineas, the Oaks and St Leger. It is a strange anomaly that fillies may, theoretically, run in all five Classic races, while colts are restricted to three, but in practice fillies almost always only run in 'their' races, the 1000 Guineas and the Oaks. (The five Classic races, and the Irish equivalent, are confined to three-year-olds only with the exception, since 1983 of the Irish St Leger, which since then has been open to all ages). At the time of *Pretty Polly* it was considered that had she been entered, she could easily have won the Derby, for she beat the top colts in subsequent races.

Tommy Lushington gave up steeplechasing to ride on the flat; it is more usually the other way round, when increasing weight forces a flat jockey to turn to jumping or give up altogether. It is all the more remarkable that this fine athlete then rode the winner of the 1900 Irish Derby on *Gallinaria*, a few short weeks after training *Ambush II* to win the Grand National for the future King of England.

Ambush fell at Navan, but won the four-mile Maiden Plate steeplechase at Punchestown in spite of refusing at the double bank; there were fourteen rivals for the four-year-old at Punchestown and it developed into a great race with *Glenartney*, a good chaser, and he won again in Leopardstown on St Stephen's (Boxing) Day. In February 1899, now a five-year-old, he won the Prince of Wales Chase at Sandown and this put him bang in the picture for the following month's Grand National, for which he started third favourite, ridden by Algy Anthony.

Another Irish 'import', Algy Anthony was born at Oxenton in Gloucestershire, on 12 June 1871. Many sources have him as being Irish, but this is not so, although most of his career was spent in Ireland. He was apprenticed to Sam Darling before going to Ireland, where he was champion jockey in 1896 and 1897. Among his biggest victories were the 1901 Stanley Steeplechase on *Drumree*, the 1911 Lancashire Chase on *The Duffrey*, and the Irish Derby twice, on *Oppressor* in 1899, and *Carrigavalla* in 1901. Also credited with training the horse, Algy Anthony rode *Ambush II* to victory in the 1900 Grand National. He was actually assistant trainer to Mr Henry Linde at Eyrefield Lodge, the Curragh, and when he finally took over the stable he saddled *Troytown* to win the 1919 Grande Steeplechase de Paris, and the 1920 Grand National. He died at Kildare in Ireland on 30 November 1923.

Ambush took to the Aintree fences and ran well in 1899, but it was the great *Manifesto's* year again. No horse deserved more to win for not only was he carrying 12st 7lbs, but also he achieved a miracle in staying on his feet when he slipped on hay placed on the landing side of the Canal Turn; equally, his rider George Williamson, performed incredible feats

to stay in the saddle. The pair then slowly but surely made up the lost ground to record a hugely popular win.

It was not the first time the Prince had attempted to win the National. His first runner was *The Scot* back in 1884, and the huge crowds who turned out to cheer him greeted the prospect of a royal runner with great excitement. *The Scot* set off in the lead and was going well when he fell at the Canal Turn last time round; as he was credited in the *Liverpool Daily Courier* with coming tenth it is quite likely that he was remounted to finish. There was still a royal connection with the winner, *Voluptuary*, who was bred at Queen Victoria's Hampton Court Stud, and had run in the 1881 Derby. A dampener was cast on the day, however, for the Prince's younger brother, Leopold, Duke of Albany, unexpectedly died.

It was the 1886 Derby that brought victory to the Prince of Wales' *Persimmon*, a talented son of the great *St Simon*. Two years later the Prince was back at Aintree when his *Magic* finished eighth behind *Playfair*. The following year, 1889, he had two runners: *Magic* who this time finished fifth behind *Frigate*, and *Hettie*, who fell.

It is perhaps no surprise that the Prince had a 'playboy' reputation. It was said that he 'liked men better than books and women better than either.' He loved company and didn't like to be alone. He associated with all sorts in pursuit of yachting, racing, gambling, shooting, travelling, playing cards, golf, and smoking cigars – as well as dalliances with Lillie Langtry in London, Hortense Schneider in Paris and various other society beauties. He was also a 'foodie' and would eat five meals a day, often of ten courses each.

But there was another side to all of this. He was brought up under an intensely strict regime, with orders given to his tutors designed to prevent him from making exactly such alliances; he was subjected to constant moral exhortation, and he received little or no display of affection from his parents when a child. He wanted to play a part in state affairs but his parents had decided early on that he had 'no intelligence or gifts of application'.

Luckily the people loved him, and his wife, Princess Alexandra of Denmark, was forgiving, tolerant, and always willing to turn a blind eye. There is a lovely print of her placing a rose in his hands as he lay on his deathbed.

In 1860, at the age of eighteen, he was allowed to go on a state visit to Canada and the United States, something of a novelty, but he quickly endeared himself to the American people – and to the pretty girls. At nineteen he was sent to Ireland on manoeuvres with the Army where fellow officers smuggled an actress into his tent. Somehow his parents found out and while Prince Albert respected him for refusing to name the officers, his mother partially blamed her consort's death a few weeks later on her son's behaviour, on the

grounds that her husband had caught a chill while on a train to visit their son to chide him once more, declaring that she 'would never be able to look at that boy without a shudder'. So perhaps it was no wonder he resorted to the good life. He undertook what public duties he could but Queen Victoria steadfastly refused to allow him to see the state papers or to act as ambassador, something that with his affability he would have been good at.

The start of the new century – the twentieth – saw the first and so far only Royal victory in the Grand National. *Ambush II* lined up again and huge crowds thronged Aintree, willing His Royal Highness's horse to win. The sixteen runners set off at a cracking pace with *Ambush* up near the front. Another Irish horse, *Covert Hack*, fell at the first fence. Then at the last Canal Turn it was the twelve-year-old *Manifesto*, burdened with 12st 13lbs who jumped spring-heeled into the lead, drawing admiring gasps of breath from the spectators. He stayed in the lead over Valentines, all the way down the back of the course, and back on to the home straight. It was not until he was between the last two fences that the veteran was caught and overtaken by *Ambush*, beautifully ridden by Algy Anthony. The hats were in the air for the Prince, but many of the cheers were also for *Manifesto*, just pipped for second on the line after his jockey eased him when hope of victory had gone. Algy Anthony went on that spring to win the Irish Oaks on *May Race*, showing his versatility in a Classic Flat race as well as in the ultimate steeplechase.

The day after the race, the Prince wrote to his son, the future George V. It gives an insight of the Prince of Wales as a father and grandfather, in contrast to the view of him presented by his own parents, and of his thrill at winning the National:

> *I trust she* [the Duchess of York who had just given birth to her third son, Prince Henry] *had a good time and is going on well and that perhaps you will be able to manage the Levee on Monday if you come up by the 9.40 train and return by 5.5. I wish you could have seen the Grand National yesterday. It really was a splendid sight, and no horse could have run faster than* Ambush. *The enthusiasm was tremendous, quite* Persimmon's *Derby over again. The weather was quite lovely. Give dear May my best love and sincerest congratulations and kiss the dear children from*
>
> *Yr Devoted Papa*
> *AE.*

He was to show similar concern for a badly injured jockey during a visit to Punchestown when he was King, insisting that the best surgeon attend him.

For the Prince of Wales his Grand National win of 1900 was the beginning of as great a run as an owner could expect, because that summer his *Diamond Jubilee* went on to win the Triple Crown of The 2000 Guineas, The Derby and The St Leger. What a way to start the new century!

Less than a month into the century's second year, in January 1901, Queen Victoria died and, aged fifty-nine, the Prince of Wales became King Edward VII. With the crown came new responsibilities – but there was no question of him giving up the Turf.

Ambush missed the next two years at Aintree, but in 1903, level at the last fence with *Drumcree*, it looked like victory for the King, only for the horse to fall there.

In 1904 his weight had gone up again, but he started favourite; this time, however, he fell at the third fence in the race won by a horse from New Zealand, *Moifaa*. *Ambush* was being prepared again for the 1905 race, but ran with lack-lustre at Sandown and then, sadly, at home on The Curragh he suffered a broken blood vessel and died. The King presented his skeleton to Liverpool Museum, without knowing that the horse's head had been removed for a post mortem, and the hooves removed in case the King should want them mounted. However, an admirable job was performed in putting the skeleton back together again. Until recent times the skeleton was in the Museum of Liverpool Life at the Pierhead. It was part of a Grand National display including a replica fence.

For the 1906 Grand National The King then bought *Moifaa* before the race; the big horse was favourite and top weight, but he fell at Becher's Brook second time round.

The King had one more runner in the Grand National, *Flaxman*, in 1908. Irish-bred and raced, he carried only 9st 12lb and started at 33-1. But the eight-year-old ran a cracking race and, but for Algy Anthony losing a stirrup at the seventeenth fence when still bang in the picture, he may well have finished closer than the creditable fourth behind *Rubio*.

The King attended the Grand National meeting in 1910 in spite of a snow squall, and waved to the cheering crowds as walked to the paddock; less than two months later, on May 6, he died, aged sixty-eight years.

6

1903 – DRUMCREE

Ballinlough Castle in County Westmeath is believed to be the longest continually lived in Irish Castle. But in the mid-1800s the son and heir, Charles Nugent, was banished to England as a 'waster'. He regularly rode in steeplechases, often under an assumed name to spare the anxiety of his mother, Letitia. One day he went through the card at Streatham, riding every winner, and another time, during a two-day meeting at Abergavenny, he rode in thirteen steeplechases.

Charles, a relation of temperance leader Father Theobald Mathew, preferred gambling and racing to turning in a day's work; when he married Emily Walker of Berkswell Hall, Warwickshire, in 1873 he sold 2,000 acres near Thurles, County Tipperary, and mortgaged another 1,000 near Mullingar, County Westmeath. He was a younger son, but his older brother was killed in a tragic shooting accident at the age of eighteen while wildfowling with school friends in Suffolk, so Charles inherited the title and castle. He was several times bankrupted, at one time having £70, a pony, and the by then dilapidated castle.

When his great-grandson John, the current baronet, and his bride, Pepe, first moved

to Lambourn in Berkshire – famous for its associations with National Hunt racehorse training – in 1959, there were two old ladies who told them how, fifty years before, Charles used to pinch their bottoms; such was his reputation.

But he did train some good racehorses, in particular *Hidden Mystery*, who won many chases, and the 'moderate' *Drumcree*, bred by Mr C. Hope and named after the horse's birthplace in Westmeath. *Hidden Mystery* had arrived in his Cranbourne, Dorset, stables 'a bag of bones', but had won in Ireland, and when Charles schooled him he discovered he was a fine jumper. More than that, in trials at home he proved so superior to other good horses that he could give them two stone and a nonchalant beating. So this was the horse that entertained live Aintree prospects, especially as he had already won a Grand Sefton Chase 'in a canter' over the fences, ridden by Charles' son, Hugh Nugent.

In 1900 he started 7-2 favourite carrying 12 stone for the 'Liverpool', as the Grand National was known in those days. Again ridden by Hugh, his was one of those genuine bad luck stories: as the horse landed over the first fence second time round a front foot went through the dangling reins of a loose horse beside him and brought him down, leaving popular victory to the Prince of Wales' Irish-trained *Ambush II*.

Sadly for *Hidden Mystery*, on a subsequent run at Sandown when shouldering a massive 14 stone, he caught his foot under the guardrail of the open ditch, broke a leg, and was put down. His brother *Leinster* was bought as a replacement and won good races, four of them at Liverpool, in a career interrupted by recurring leg problems.

So when *Drumcree* came along, he was not rated in the same breath as these equine brothers and he was quirky, too, for he was near impossible to get to enter his stable, and on occasions refused to come out of it, a relic from a time when a hen jumped up squawking and startled him as he was going in, causing him to hit his head on a beam. He spent one night in a coach house rather than go in to his stable; and another time it took thirty-six hours to cajole him to come out, in spite of corn and carrots and other food and titbits being left outside to try and lure him.

Drumcree was a bay gelding, quite tall, with a big white star on a kind head and good bone. He was by *Ascetic*, a stallion who also sired Grand National winners *Ascetic's Silver* (1906), and the great *Cloister* who won the 1893 race carrying 12st 7lbs. Built in the mould of *Troytown, Cloister* was the '*beau ideal*' of a big, powerful steeplechaser, described as possessing 'beautifully laid shoulders, great depth through the chest, a clearly defined jumping bone, and muscular quarters with remarkable length from great square hips to big well-formed hocks.' He was a hard puller, ran with his head low, and won in the then record time of nine minutes, 32.2/5 seconds (or 42.2/5 in some reports) on ground that was described as 'very hard and dry' in 'sunny and hot' weather.

Drumcree was set to carry Hugh Nugent in the 1901 National. This time the going was described as 'very deep – course white with snow', and the weather as 'blinding snowstorm'. It is hardly surprising that the stewards thought long and hard about running the race – some of the jockeys asked them not to let it go ahead, but go ahead it did in the end. It was the ingenuity of owner Bernard Bletsoe that won the day for *Grudon*; Bletsoe, who also bred and trained the horse, went out and bought some pounds of butter that he then pressed into *Grudon*'s feet. As a result, the snow did not 'ball' and, unlike his rivals who were slipping and sliding all over the place, he was able to jump and gallop safely to a convincing all-the-way win.

Drumcree, who had won his previous two races, was an honourable runner up four lengths behind having spread a plate (that is, lost a shoe) and another one having twisted, causing a tricky disadvantage. The following year, carrying nearly a stone more, he could manage only seventh, behind one of just thirteen mares ever to have won the race, *Shannon Lass*. Bred in County Clare by James Reidy, she ran third in a Limerick chase as a three-year-old before finding herself in the ownership of an English bookmaker. *Drumcree* made the early running and was there with every chance until fading over the last few fences.

For 1903, however, Charles Nugent had 'tried' *Drumcree* for the great race by galloping him over two miles on the flat and straight on into another two miles over fences. He was sure he would win and, although his weight had gone up to 11st 3lb, *Drumcree* started 13-2 favourite in a field of twenty-three. The going was good and the weather perfect. Imagine the disappointment, therefore, for Hugh Nugent when he broke a collarbone shortly before the race. Aintree's history is littered with such stories, the bad luck for the intended rider becoming the good luck for the substitute who goes on and wins. In this case it was twenty-

one-year-old Percy Woodland, who was to find himself in exactly the same lucky shoes ten years later on *Covertcoat*, following an injury to Ernie Piggott.

In 1903, the mighty *Manifesto* was fifteen years old, yet still set to carry 12st 3lb, but it was *Drumcree*'s race. *Ambush* set sail in front ahead of a lot of fallers; even so, heading for the last there was a group of six in close contention, just headed by *Drumcree*. *Drumree* (a different horse to *Drumcree*) and *Kirkland* were closing and gallant *Manifesto* was not out of it yet but suddenly *Drumree* fell on the flat, in almost as mysterious a fashion as was to happen to the Queen Mother's Irish-bred *Devon Loch* fifty-three years later. One fence was left and here, making his challenge, *Ambush* fell, denying the king of the realm his second victory. *Drumcree* jumped the fence perfectly and ran out a worthy three-length winner.

Hugh Nugent had now filled the runner's up berth, and watched 'his' ride win from the sidelines. But sadly true tragedy lay ahead. He was due to ride in Ostend; his pregnant wife begged him not to go, for she dreamed she saw a coffin with candles round it and nuns praying. Hugh went and rode the horse, *Red Dragon of Wales*, for owner Mr Belton in the Full Cry hurdle race. He took a fall, landed on his head, and was killed. Hugh junior was born posthumously months later.

Years later, visiting the cemetery, he asked the curator where the grave of Hugh Nugent was.

'Over there,' came the immediate response.

'How on earth do you know?'

The curator replied,

'I've never forgotten – I was a little boy standing at the fence where he was killed.'

Sir Charles was, naturally, devastated by the death of his only son. After a gap of three years *Drumcree* ran twice more in the National, in 1906 when he finished eighth behind

Ascetic's Silver and in 1907 when he fell in the race won by *Eremon*. Owned by a wealthy South African, Mr J.S. Morrison, it is believed that *Drumcree* was buried in Durban.

When Sir Charles died in 1927, Ballinlough Castle, which had been lived in by his sister and his cousin and family, was nearly derelict. Charles' grandson, Hugh, inherited it. His mother, widowed after Hugh senior's death in the hurdle accident, remarried a man from Kent, one Edwin John King who had sold his shipping fleet to Union Castle. It was he who gave Hugh junior, the castle's new incumbent, £10,000 to restore it. But more than that, Hugh also had to regain the castle itself, yard, woods and eighty acres that had been requisitioned by the Land Commission. He managed to get more of the original demesne land back, too, by buying outlying farms and persuading castle land incumbents to swap.

Eventually Hugh's son John and wife, Pepe, came to the castle, after a long career in Lambourn where they not only continued the transport and horsebox manufacturing business started by Hugh (the familiar LRT, Lambourn Racehorse Transport), but also in the upkeep of the gallops. With John and Pepe now 'retired' into the Stewards House – along with *Drumcree*'s portrait, mounted hoof (small and slender) and jockey's whip – it is their son Nick, Sales and Marketing Director and one of the chief auctioneers at Goffs, and family, that are resident in the castle.

Bloodstock, like the castle, remains very much in the family.

1920 – TROYTOWN;
1939 – WORKMAN

Of all the marvellous winners of the Grand National, *Troytown* has to be one of the greatest. He towered over his rivals and ran them ragged. Had not *Poethlyn*, victor of the previous two Grand Nationals, been running, *Troytown* would undoubtedly have started favourite as he had won the previous summer's French Grand National at Auteuil.

Poethlyn was after that elusive accolade of three Grand National wins. As his first was at the Wartime substitute course at Gatwick there were inevitably those that dismissed his effort – though the organisers had done their best to imitate the real thing by increasing the size of the fences. That he came to Aintree and won over the real course carrying 12st 7lbs in 1919 rubber-stamped his ability.

Troytown was bred near to Navan Racecourse in County Meath where he is well commemorated. The Troytown Chase is run there every November and is an accepted Grand National trial. There is also an amazing painted and framed tribute to him in which it is said that every square inch contains twenty-five colours. It now hangs in the clubroom and is well worth looking at, for the sheer painstaking work alone.

His breeder was Major Thomas Collins-Gerrard of Fitzherbert Estate, Gibbstown, which in those days covered two thousand acres. The major retained ownership of *Troytown*, and sent him to Eyrefield Lodge on the Curragh, home of the late Harry Eyre Linde, for training by Algy Anthony.

Troytown was a very tall, angular chaser, a good 17 hands high, with a star on his forehead the same shape as the one that *Mill House* was to be born with. He was otherwise brown all over, bar a little mealy around his nostrils; he had long ears, a raking stride, and he possessed a great zest for life. He was described in Con O'Leary's 1945 book about the National as, 'more than 17 hands high, bone and muscle in proportion, a clean and bony head, fine shoulders, great depth of heart, powerful back and loins, and a kind eye.'

He was only six years old when he won both the Grande Steeplechase de Paris at Auteuil and the Champion Chase at Aintree. He came to the Grand National with a huge amount of Irish confidence on him; he had won over the Aintree fences and his two most recent races.

Algy Anthony was champion jockey in Ireland in 1896 and 1897. Among his biggest victories were the 1900 Grand National on *Ambush II*, the 1901 Stanley Steeplechase on *Drumree*, the 1911 Lancashire Chase on *The Duffrey*, and the Irish Derby twice, on *Oppressor* in 1899, and *Carrigavalla* in 1901. He was also credited with training *Ambush II* from Eyrefield Lodge, the Curragh.

The ease with which he mixed and matched riding on the flat and over fences is further illustrated in that he also won two Irish Oaks, and two Galway Plates, the latter being Ireland's big summer handicap steeplechase, the jewel in the crown of what is now a week-long racing festival.

When he began training it was firstly from Eyrefield Lodge and latterly at Westenra, also on The Curragh, from where he saddled *Troytown* to win the 1919 Grande Steeplechase de Paris, and the 1920 Grand National.

He was almost as successful a trainer as he had been a rider. Taking a leaf out of his mentor, Linde's, book and those of a few others, he built a schooling course of steeplechase fences on his training grounds at Westenra. It meant that his horses were always well schooled before they first went jumping in public, *Troytown* being the most famous one.

March 26, 1920 was one of those days when the rain poured down, the ground became 'bottomless' and it was so murky that little could be seen of the twenty-four runners as they lined up for the Grand National. In *Troytown*'s saddle was Jack Anthony, bidding for his third success in the race.

Jack (no relation to Algy) had twice previously written himself on to the roll of honour. In 1911 it was via *Glenside*, an Irish-bred gelding that was blind in one eye and had wind trouble; he had been brought down by a stable companion in the previous year's race and now, ridden by Grand National debutant Jack Anthony, was the only horse to complete the course without falling. Jack won again in 1915 on *Ally Sloper*, the last National to be run at Aintree until 1919.

Now, in 1920, his prowess in the saddle was needed more than ever before because right from the start *Troytown* powered his way into the lead. Behind him the anticipated duel with *Poethlyn* ended prematurely when *Poethlyn* joined the list of previous winners to fall at the first fence. Before long, others were littering the ground as well.

The rain did not help Jack Anthony's cause for it made the reins slippery and therefore difficult to hold firmly and, ergo, to control the horse. In racing parlance, he was a passenger. Nevertheless, his skill was still called for, especially at the penultimate fence where *Troytown* virtually disregarded it and galloped straight through. The racing wags of the time all voiced the opinion that an inferior horse would have fallen, or a lesser jockey would have been unseated. It did let in *The Bore* who was able to range up alongside and actually overtake the big horse. But *Troytown* was not for beating. Showing the sort of courage and tenacity that separates the great from the good, he powered on with such effect that it was some way beyond the winning post before Algy Anthony could pull him up – and that at the end of 4½ miles, thirty of the world's most awesome fences – and in atrocious conditions.

Afterwards, his rider was quoted as saying his mount was 'more of a steam engine than a racehorse.'

The world was now *Troytown*'s oyster. He was only seven years old and was already the winner of the Grand National and France's biggest chase, too. A few months later he returned to Paris – after the ferry was delayed for some days by striking French dock workers (so what's new!) – for another crack at the Grande Steeplechase de Paris, and he finished third. He remained in France for six days to run in the Prix des Drags.

Auteuil is a beautiful, green, park-like setting in Paris and its steeplechase course has a variety of fences, more like some of the fences now found on the cross-country courses at Cheltenham and Punchestown. They can take some adapting to for English and Irish horses used only to regular birch steeplechase fences, but *Troytown* had already proved himself over them, so there won't have been any more than normal nerves about running him there again. Sadly, in one of those errors that remind us all too potently that horses are not machines, *Troytown* misjudged one of the smaller fences on the course, came down and regrettably had to be put down. He broke a bone above his knee.

One story that has come down the years is that rather than risk him becoming meat on French dinner plates he was buried. A large tomb with a moving epitaph was erected to him in the dog cemetery at Asnières, and can still be seen today.

Troytown would come into the top five of many aficionados' Grand National lists, not least Jane Clarke, curator of the museum at Aintree.

She says,

'I would always choose *Troytown* in my top five, firstly, for his obvious ability, his power and his game, genuine look. He appeared to simply toy with the huge Aintree fences. If you read accounts from that time, it is crystal clear how highly he was considered by all those who knew about horses. All were in agreement that he was something special with tremendous potential.

'Secondly, I think the tragedy of his death in France at such a young age makes him even more of an icon to me. I have read Jack Anthony's heartbreaking description of how he felt immediately after the accident when he found himself all alone with the stricken horse – and have been in tears over it. His owner loved him so much that he had him buried in the pets' cemetery at Asnières and the inscription on his tomb – "Troytown, Darling"– says it all.'

Only three years later, Algy Anthony, too, died, after a long illness, on 30 November 1923.

◆ ◆ ◆

The one hundredth winner of the Grand National was Ireland's *Workman*, owned by Englishman Sir Alexander Maguire an industrialist whose business in manufacturing matches took him to Dublin and Belfast as well as Liverpool. Jack Ruttle trained *Workman* at Hazlehatch near Celbridge, on the border of Counties Kildare and Dublin.

A brown gelding by *Cottage*, *Workman* was bred by Mr P.J. O'Leary, of Charleville, County Cork in 1930. He was the first of three Grand National winners by *Cottage*, the others being *Lovely Cottage*, 1946, and *Sheila's Cottage*, 1948.

Amateur rider R. de L. Stedman purchased him and together they won the 1936 La Touche Cup at Punchestown. In 1937 he not only sold him to Sir Alexander, presumably for good money, but also kept the ride on him in the Irish Grand National in which he finished third.

He rounded off the 1936/37 season by finishing third in the Conyngham Cup Handicap Chase at Punchestown on 28 April 1937. He won first time out in the 1937/38 season in the Webster Cup Handicap Chase at Navan on 11 September 1937 ridden by Jimmy Brogan (whose son, Barry, may be best remembered for his association with *The Dikler*), but then fell in the Grand Sefton Handicap Chase at Aintree in November. *Workman* then won the Stillorgan Handicap Chase at Leopardstown on 19 February 1938, the year *Workman* first ran in the Grand National, again ridden by the professional Jimmy Brogan. For many years, from 1915 until 2000, the Brogan family ran Brogan's Hotel in Trim, County Meath, where a picture of *Workman* used to hang; it is now with Denys Merrick and his wife, Geraldine, a first cousin of Jimmy.

The 1938 Grand National, in which *Workman* finished third, was an epic. He almost joined the leaders *Royal Danieli* and *Battleship* four out, but could not sustain the challenge. This saw one of the closest ever finishes between the first two, the verdict going by a head to the tiny full horse, *Battleship*, ridden by Bruce Hobbs, at seventeen still the youngest winning jockey in the history of the race. The Irish horse, *Royal Danieli*, ridden by Dan Moore, put his all into the race and never seemed quite the same again in later years.

The 1938/39 season started off badly for *Workman* when he fell in the Galway Plate on 27 July 1938, but he soon made amends when he finished second in the Troytown Handicap Chase at Punchestown that October. Sir Alexander began to dream more seriously of the National, even more so when his horse finished fourth to *Rockquilla* over the fences in the Grand Sefton, and then ran second in the Stillorgan chase at Leopardstown in February, a month before the National.

Now, when it mattered most, he was to get even better.

Jack Ruttle had been a good jockey for the Harty family in County Limerick, and had already tasted top training success with *Halston* in 1922 when he added an Irish Grand National at Fairyhouse to two Conynham Cups at Punchestown; he also trained a Classic winner in *Santaria*, who won the Irish Oaks of 1932. He had a hunch about *Workman*: he was convinced that the man to get the best out of him was a show-jumper named Tim Hyde, so he set about enticing him away from his successful career in that discipline to take up steeplechasing – with remarkable results.

Tim Hyde finished the 1937 season as joint leading amateur and turned professional the following year when he won the Irish National on *Clare County* beating Tom Dreaper on *My Branch*.

Before the 1939 Grand National *Workman* was the 'talking horse', that is, the one that the newspapers and gossips latched on to as the likely winner. He had only gone up 4lbs in the weights since the previous year and there was a lot of Irish confidence in him. One can imagine the stable lads 'helping themselves' to bets at generous odds, and although the favourite was Dorothy Paget's *Kilstar*, the hoped-for successor to the Irish-bred *Golden Miller*, (winner of an unprecedented five Cheltenham Gold Cups and a Grand National), *Workman's* odds came in to be fourth favourite, along with *Danieli* and 1937 winner *Royal Mail*.

In the race it looked as if *Kilstar* might emulate his owner's great predecessor and he was still leading over the second Becher's. By this time, poor *Danieli* and Dan Moore had taken a horrendous fall and a number of others were also out of the race. That is part of the allure of the National, the knowing that a certain number will fall by the wayside, the not knowing who, and the hoping that it won't be your own bet…

Kilstar continued to lead but *Black Hawk* and a Scottish horse, *Macmoffat*, were now closing in on him, and creeping ever nearer – in workmanlike fashion – was *Workman*.

He joined the leaders at the last Valentines but, leaping over the twenty-seventh fence, collided in mid air with *Black Hawk*. It was *Workman* who fared best, and *Black Hawk* was knocked to the ground while *Workman* strode on and cleared the last in the lead. On that long, long run-in *Macmoffat* challenged, drawing ever closer, but *Workman* held on for a fine three-length win from *Macmoffat*, with *Kilstar* back in third.

Macmoffat was again to fill the runner's up berth in 1940 (to *Bogskar*), with *Danieli* again a faller and *Kilstar* only twelfth, while *Workman* did not run in the National again, his record being third and first. It was the last Grand National at Aintree until after the War in 1946.

One of the great traditions for a Grand National winner, especially an Irish one, is its home-coming, and *Workman* was no exception. It was not too far from the Dublin docks to Celbridge, and the Johnstown, Hazelhatch Bridge stables of Jack Ruttle. The kitchen staff there ensured everyone would be able to dance the night away by taking a number of doors off their hinges and laying them on the ground in the yard, thus making an impromptu dance floor!

History does not relate whether Sir Alexander Maguire, sixty-three years old at the time of this victory, was also there to join in the celebrations, but once he retired from the Liverpool business founded by his father he retired to a somnambulant life on the South Coast of England in Eastbourne, Sussex.

Tim Hyde was 'headhunted' for the second time when Tom Dreaper enticed him to be his stable jockey. While Tim won the Grand National with *Workman*, it is for not winning it on *Prince Regent*, try as they might, that he is often remembered. He did, of course, win both the Cheltenham Gold Cup and the Irish National on *Prince Regent*, and, but for the war, there are many convinced that he would also have won a National. He also won the Galway Plate for Tom Dreaper on *Keep Faith*.

Tim Hyde suffered the cruellest luck when, attending a show, he was involved in an accident that paralysed him and left him in a wheelchair. He was the father of Timmy Hyde, best known as a buyer of bloodstock, whose daughters married jockeys/trainers Norman Williamson and Charlie Swan.

8

1947 – CAUGHOO

THE WORST WINTER ON RECORD – and possibly worse than 1962-3, which also went down in the annals as harsh – 1946-47 saw snow still lying on the ground in mid-March, more than three months since the initial fall in the UK. There had been no thaw in between, hardly any let up. It was nearly as bad in Ireland where racing was also cancelled.

Among the trades and professions for whom this caused extra headaches were racehorse trainers. Long before the days of all-weather gallops, the most a trainer was likely to do was lay a straw ring around which horses could trot, laying the soiled straw from out of the stables instead of putting it on the muck heap. Those who lived close enough to the sea could exercise on sand beaches – if they could get there.

In those days jockeys were paid per ride; there was no wage or salary, precious few retainers, and no benevolent funds. It was a case of no racing, no income.

One effect of the Big Freeze was that the Grand National would now, most unusually, be run before Cheltenham, as the NH Festival had been postponed to April from mid-March. The Liverpool date was 29 March 1947 and, with owners and trainers doubtless as keen as the jockeys to get a run at last, fifty-seven horses were declared, the second biggest field ever in the National's history (after *Gregalach*'s 1929 win from a field of sixty-six).

In 1947 there were without doubt a number of no-hopers. After all, how could they be taken seriously against the mighty *Prince Regent* and a host of other horses with promise: *Sheila's Cottage* was to win the next year; *Silver Fame* was to win twenty-four races including a Cheltenham Gold Cup and become, still in 2008, the horse to win more races at Cheltenham than any other; *Revelry* was also fancied, but most of the runners were on huge prices. Even 1940 winner *Bogskar*, now fourteen years old, was priced at 100-1. Others also with fair credentials were overlooked in such a large, competitive field, including Irish eight-year-old, *Caughoo*.

This was a horse that had already won two Ulster Grand Nationals at Downpatrick, County Down, another course that, like Aintree, is a law unto itself; it is so steeply undulating that it's been compared to a funfair switchback ride.

The sea was to play a large part in the brown gelding's life. He was bred by Patrick Power at Fethard-on-Sea, County Wexford, and was to be trained on the Bull Wall, in Clontarf, North Dublin and then, after Herbert McDowell moved house, on the beach between Portmarnock and Malahide, not far from the now defunct Baldoyle racecourse.

Caughoo was bred for the flat; by *Within The Law*, who bred some winning two-year-olds, he was out of the sprinter *Silverdale*, also bred by Power, but although she barely got five furlongs she won eight 'little' races; she traced to *Black Duchess*, known as one of the greatest mares in the Stud Book, in the same line as *Gainsborough* and *Hyperion*. *Silverdale* was by *Vencedor*, who was by *Orby*, Ireland's first colt to win both the Epsom and Irish Derbies in 1907.

As a two-year-old, *Caughoo* was sent to the Ballsbridge Sales where Herbert McDowell, a vet, bought him on the advice of his friend and mentor, fellow vet Jack White, for only 50 guineas; later on in the story he sold him to his brother, Dublin jeweller, Mr J.J. 'Jack' McDowell, and he was always a 'family horse.' They named the horse *Caughoo* after their father's estate in County Cavan. Being able to train on the sandy beach during the freeze was of huge benefit, because he was able to continue working (galloping and cantering), while others less fortunate were confined to a hastily laid straw ring to walk or at best trot round.

Walk down O'Connell Street in Dublin today and there is McDowell's jewellers – the 'Happy Ring House' – take a closer look, and the 1947 Grand National trophy, a small gold cup, can be seen there. The shop was founded in 1870 by John McDowell, and later owned by his brother, Willie. It was probably in Mary Street until 1902 when it moved to O'Connell Street.

The shop was flattened in the riots of 1916 and much of the stock was looted. Willie

made a dash for the train in Amiens Street to get home; the station porter was shot dead; Willie himself received a pellet in the leg.

'But,' says the current John McDowell, 'the British Government paid compensation within three weeks, and the premises were rebuilt using girders from the destroyed Post Office building.'

Willie died suddenly one day when in the barber's shop and J.J. 'Jack' McDowell took over. A third brother Cecil, father of the current John, was an orthopaedic surgeon who won a few point-to-points, but died aged forty-nine.

Today the men at the helm are John and his cousin Peter McDowell, son of Herbert.

Caughoo's early racing record did not bode well. He was so useless in flat races, finishing unplaced every time, that his jockey, Morney Wing, jokingly advised Herbert to shoot him. There was a story after his National victory that the horse had at one time suffered an ailment and the McDowells had been advised to put him down. I suspect that the 'ailment' was a 'touch of the slows' and the near-death was the jockey's comment.

The horse was schooled over hurdles, found he could leap and he finished third in the Galway Hurdle. Before long he had won the Ulster Grand National of 1945, and a good offer was turned down for him; instead, Herbert sold him to his brother, Jack. Jack was

'FITTER THAN EVER,' HE STILL
LOVES TO BE AT THE SEASIDE

Grand National acceptances were announced last night. Among them are five Irish-trained horses—Caughoo, Sagacity, Anaubes, Ardnacassa and Loyal Antrim.

Again and again an Irish horse comes from nowhere to win Aintree's Blue Riband. JOHN GODLEY is back in London after a week in Ireland, where he visited the small stables which have a National entrant. This week he will tell readers what he found. Here is the story of CAUGHOO, the 1947 National winner.

GRASS gallops were frozen solid during weeks of frosty weather two years ago, trainer Bertie McDowell, of Malahide, Co. Dublin, Eire, took his brother's horse Caughoo to exercise on the sandy seashore at Portmarnock, nearby.

Caughoo liked to be beside the seaside, and said that you in March, 1947, by winning the Grand National 100-1.

This year the ground's not hard, but Caughoo still gallops on Portmarnock beach. "He loves it," says Bert "He'll be fitter for this year's National than ever bef —and a better horse."

I spent a morning watching Caughoo at work. Fir he was ridden INTO the sea, where he "paddled" for t minutes.

"Good for the legs," said Bertie.

Then Caughoo and stable companion Tonight's t Night—also owned by Bertie's brother Jack—set off slo the beach for a two-mile gallop at half speed.

Riding Caughoo was stable-boy Ted Wright. After his

popular locally and played rugby for the Suttonians; he registered his racing colours in the royal blue, green and white of the club, and Herbert continued the training.

The only horses stabled with *Caughoo* were *Warren Lad*, who had won fourteen point-to-points in his time, and *Marcelbert*, a show-jumper who had won the Championship Jumping Competition at the Dublin Spring Show a few years previously; and so it was that *Caughoo* was often seen alone on the sands, especially during the big freeze. Racehorses are usually 'worked' in 'strings', that is, several horses in line, or maybe two or three abreast. *Caughoo* enjoyed striding out on the beach, and he loved it at the end when, stripped of his saddle, he was allowed to roll, while 'lad' Ted Wright, who looked after him 'night and day', hung on to the reins. Ted Wright's son, Eddie, became a jockey with Jim Dreaper, being mainly associated with *Colebridge*.

In spite of his Flat breeding, *Caughoo* won back-to-back Ulster Nationals in 1945 and 1946. The family debated whether to tackle the Grand National at Aintree or to bid for a hat-trick in Ulster. One friend, Jack Cox, father of leading amateur Bunny, advised they would be mad to try anything other than Downpatrick. But the brothers had faith in their horse. Small he might be, but he had shown he had stature. To demonstrate their conviction, they arranged for a string of 'runners' to go down the line of bookmakers at Aintree, placing a tenner each on the horse. Even so, it was not enough to dent the market, and *Caughoo* remained one of the twenty-six runners to start at 100-1; 250-1 on the Tote.

Apart from one elderly farmer in County Clare, there was little other support for *Caughoo* on either side of the water. The eighty-three-year-old from Ennis had such a vivid dream that he placed £30 on the horse. When *Caughoo* won he felt so guilty at having 'taken' £3,000 when he 'knew' the result in advance, that he sent £1,000 to the Pope to aid starving children. Naturally local people supported 'their' horse, however, and the local bookmaker in Howth was wiped out of business by the success of the horse; later the winning owner, Jack McDowell, set him up again.

The weather on race morning was so bad that Aer Lingus was unable to fly from Dublin to Liverpool and forty would-be spectators, the *Irish Independent* photographer among them, were stranded.

But in Liverpool itself the crowds flocked in. The first Saturday National for eighty-nine years, spectators began arriving at daybreak and, travelling by whatever means they could in the pouring rain, they were soon said to be numbering 100,000 per hour; newspapers variously reported the crowd as being 300,000, 400,000, even half a million. There were six hundred policemen and thirty patrol cars marshalling them on to the course; and a plane circled overhead issuing directions.

When *Caughoo*'s jockey Eddie Dempsey arrived at the course not only were the huge fences strange to him, but it was also the first time he had ever set foot in England; nevertheless he rode a remarkably cool, intelligent race. At thirty-five years old he was, in racing parlance 'aged' and in fact he was already semi-retired; he had not ridden a winner for three years, the last one being *Never No More* at Baldoyle on St Patrick's Day, 17 March 1944. Born and bred in Macetown, between Tara and Gibbstown in County Meath, he now lived not far away at The Ward, County Dublin. Eddie had been headman to Tom Dreaper from 1941-44 where he was the first to ride and win on *Prince Regent*. His uncle, Patrick Dempsey, broke in and trained the marvellous 1920 Grand National winner, *Troytown*.

Of the nine horses that had travelled over from Ireland many were better fancied than *Caughoo*, notably the favourite – of punters and people – *Prince Regent*, even though he was now twelve years old and set to shoulder 12st 7lbs; it was twenty years since the favourite had last won the race, *Sprig* in 1927, the year the race was first broadcast on radio.

It has often been said that World War II prevented *Prince Regent* from winning the National, but there is also the possibility that he did not truly stay out the distance; what might have been had there been Grand Nationals during the War years can only remain conjecture. Certainly he carried all before him in his native Ireland. Trained by Tom Dreaper for J.V. Rank he did attain the highest chasing crown by winning the 1942 Irish Grand National and, after the War, the 1946 Cheltenham Gold Cup, aged eleven years. Understandably there are many who believe he could have won all the war years' Gold Cups had they been staged; it is also an oft-told story that Tom Dreaper could not for a long time rate *Arkle* ahead of his earlier prince. That *Arkle* was the king became undisputed, but *Prince Regent* was more than a very, very good horse. With age against him after the War, he finished third in the 1946 Grand National and fourth in 1947, ridden in both by Tim Hyde and carrying 12st 5lbs and 12st 7lbs respectively. As a thirteen-year-old in 1948, on 12st 2lb, he was carried out (that is, a loose horse swerved across him in front of a fence, forcing him out of the race).

Tom Dreaper's trademark was patience and it was not until *Prince Regent* was five years old that he saw a racecourse, winning a flat race at Naas ridden by Tom Dreaper himself. The next year, in 1941, he won a hurdle race in Phoenix Park and then his first chases at Dundalk and Navan. The Irish Grand National was among his four wins of 1942 even though he had to carry 12st 7lbs. Luckily, *Prince Regent* was a spanking big horse, well able to take the weights that were meted out to him during his career.

The afternoon of the 1947 Grand National was misty after the heavy rain. Amateur rider (that is, a jockey who is unpaid to ride, his income comes from elsewhere) John Hislop, who was to write the 'bible' on how to ride in steeplechases, was on board a small French horse, *Kami.* In the vein of John Lawrence (later Lord Oaksey) to follow him, he wrote an account of the race from the saddle for the *Observer* which, with the visibility so poor for the hacks in the stands, may be the most accurate record.

His description of the start rings true today, and is especially reminiscent of 2007. He wrote, 'As usual there was much scrimmaging and restiveness at the start with the starter shouting 'keep off the tapes'!

'*The gates went up and we jumped off, most of us as eagerly as if we had five furlongs to go. Kami couldn't go the pace but he jumped perfectly and got into a rhythm.*'

The second favourite *Revelry* fell at the first giving a nasty fall to Dan Moore, who was stretchered off with a neck injury; Martin Molony was brought down on *E.P.* while *Revelry* continued on his own to jump every fence. By the first Becher's half a dozen were riderless. *Caughoo* was nearly amongst them; he pitched on his nose over the first three fences but then got the hang of those unfamiliar obstacles and remained foot perfect thereafter, one of those to adapt to and then relish the experience.

Off they disappeared into the mist and by the time they came back into view it was an

Irish horse, *Lough Conn*, who was bowling along in the lead, a circuit completed behind them. *Prince Regent* had also blundered at the third fence and then, just when he was clawing his way back into the race, he was hampered by a loose horse at the Chair.

Caughoo was being given a patient ride by Eddie Dempsey and was among the second group along with *Prince Regent* as they literally disappeared again into the country. *Lough Conn* was still loving the experience and led by ten lengths; by the time they reached Valentines both *Prince Regent* and *Caughoo* were improving rapidly, but poor *Silver Fame* was put out by a loose horse. A class horse that was to win the Cheltenham Gold Cup in 1951, Aintree was not for him.

When the remaining runners re-emerged out of the mist, *Lough Conn* was also hampered by a loose horse and it was *Caughoo* who swept into the lead from his compatriot.

John Hislop takes it up again:

'*Coming back over the* [Melling] *road with two to jump,* Prince Regent *in front of me was visibly tiring, and still a good way ahead was the green jacket of* Lough Conn *and the green and blue of the eventual winner of whose identity I was as ignorant as, I suppose, the majority of spectators.*'

This was true, for it is said spectators hurriedly looked at their cards to try and identify this horse storming out of the gloom and heading for glory. The little horse put twenty lengths between himself and gallant *Lough Conn* in what was the slowest time for twenty years. *Kami* overtook *Prince Regent*; this meant that three unusually small horses had performed best in the atrocious underfoot conditions, contradicting the long held adage of the National 'type' as being 'a big hunter for the big fences'.

It was said that *Lough Conn*'s jockey, Dan McCann, apparently accused Eddie Dempsey of having waited in the mist and rejoined fresh on the second circuit. A photograph of *Caughoo* jumping the water jump in front of the stands at the end of the first circuit refutes that beyond doubt. Also, Peter McDowell owns two photographs of him jumping Becher's twice: there are clearly different horses around him on each occasion; nevertheless the story goes that McCann went to his grave believing he had been 'robbed'.

Lough Conn was another family horse and had cost even less than *Caughoo*, trainer Frank Boland, son of local auctioneer W. Boland, having bought him for just 30 guineas as a yearling in Ballsbridge; he then brought him home to Ballina, County Mayo to pull the plough, a task he sometimes continued to perform between races. Like *Caughoo*, he was never 'in a great training stable or prepared on orthodox gallops'. In 1944 he 'ran away' with the Punchestown Cup; he ran in the first post War Grand National displaying his front running tactics until falling on the second circuit at a fence with a big gap made through it first time round.

Caughoo came home to a splendid Irish reception, but after a day's delay; he was prevented from embarking on the ferry at Holyhead because his export licence was not available, and the latest Grand National hero had to spend the night in a stable normally reserved for the railway company's carthorse!

The McDowells took the first ferry home and ensured a fantastic journey for all the passengers as, waving their victorious colours aloft, the order was 'drinks all round'. They drank the bar dry and went into the Guinness Book of Records as having hosted the biggest 'round' ever. They returned to the next Aintree meeting some weeks later to pick up their winnings – one bookmaker tried to renege, but the course detective made him pay up. They lodged an offshore account in Liverpool that is believed to have been 'well used.' Jack's betting winnings came to about £12,500, and his prize money was £9,932, a very big sum for the time.

Once *Caughoo* and the other horses landed safely, docker Jack Simpson – who had led *Caughoo* to his ferry, the LMS ss Slievemore, on the outward journey – was granted permission to lead him off. Then it was over to his regular lad, Ted Wright.

The streets were lined with well-wishers all along the Quays, on O'Connell Bridge and up O'Connell Street where those trying to get the best view scaled statues and climbed on top of trams and Guinness tenders, and some even erected telescopic ladders. A special force of police was on duty to clear the way, ensuring cart ponies, drag horses and asses on the road made way; and a 'battery of cameras' clicked away.

The Emerald Girl Pipers' Band and the James Stephens Pipers' Band led the parade, playing 'stirring martial airs.'

Caughoo himself enjoyed the crowds and fuss, prancing and kicking to the cheering crowds, responding to the three cheers given for him.

Later in the week, Jack McDowell gave a victory party for about three hundred in the Gresham Hotel, Dublin, after which Eddie Dempsey was escorted in a big procession of cars to Ashbourne and to his home-place at The Wooton. Bonfires burned along the route and houses were decorated with the National flag and with *Caughoo's* colours. His employer, Mrs Whitmore, presented Eddie with a gold watch in honour of his great victory. The event was organised by the Dongahmore Football Club, members of the Ward Union Hunt, and the Greenogue and Killsallaghan training stables 'and other friends of the winning jockey.'

Another reception and gala dinner was held in the Marine Hotel, Sutton, while after the race in Liverpool Jack McDowell had been the main toast at the customary dinner dance, with Eddie Dempsey also at the table.

During that summer *Caughoo* was to get well used to parading, at shows in Dublin, Balmoral, Cork, Cavan, Dundalk and so on. But first he ran in another race, three weeks after the National, at his local Baldoyle. The crowds flocked to it, but *Caughoo*, so soon after his Aintree exertions, could finish only third, his jockey declining to use the whip on him after the horse had achieved the ultimate chasing prize. Nevertheless, the stewards called in both trainer and jockey to account for the 'failed' performance.

Caughoo ran in the 1948 Grand National, but was pulled up at the twenty-third fence; in 1949 he ran out at the fifth fence whilst ridden by Daniel McCann.

He lived out his life in the gentle retirement he deserved at a farm owned by Jack McDowell's mother, Caroline, and died peacefully; he was buried at Sutton until a number of years later when the land was developed for building. *Caughoo's* remains were exhumed and reburied on the farm opposite Fairyhouse Racecourse, then owned by Peter McDowell. That was sold later to Tattersalls (Ireland) Bloodstock Sales when Peter and his family moved to Headford, Kells, but happily the grave of *Caughoo* remains undisturbed in the garden in front of the house.

Among the memorabilia in John McDowell's home, overlooking the River Boyne, is an exquisite silk scarf, framed, showing *Caughoo* jumping at Aintree as the central piece, and surrounded by shield-like name plates of all the previous winners up to his year of 1947.

The current McDowells keep a few brood mares and bred 1991 Cheltenham Gold Cup winner, *Garrison Savannah*.

Peter McDowell owns the emerald green and royal blue halved colours, with white sleeves and cap, unwashed since the day of the victory, and he has loaned them, along with the bridle worn on the winning day, to the museum in Malahide Castle; he still has the original trainer's cup.

9

1953 – EARLY MIST;
1954 – ROYAL TAN;
1955 – QUARE TIMES

IT IS SAID THAT MILLING MAGNATE Mr. J.V. 'Jimmy' Rank, one of Tom Dreaper's principal patrons, had three sporting ambitions: to win the Derby, the Waterloo Cup, and the Grand National. He narrowly failed; he finished second in all three, but not only that, just over a year after his death, his former horse *Early Mist* won the Grand National.

It was a sad day in January 1952 when Mr Rank died, and poignant on Irish Derby Day on the Curragh the following June for the dispersal sale of his horses.

He had won the Cheltenham Gold Cup with *Prince Regent* and that is the pinnacle, the 'Derby', of the NH tree because it is played out at level weights; but he would also have felt denied of the Grand National with his star because of the war years when no National was run.

Early Mist was bred in England and sold at the Newmarket Sales as a yearling to an Irish buyer; he was then re-sold at Ballsbridge Sales, Dublin, for 625 guineas to J.V. Rank. He was a washy (pale) chestnut with a narrow white stripe down his face.

Right from the start of his racing career the strapping big chestnut showed ability, winning all four races in his first season, and then progressing to win chases at Naas, Fairyhouse and Leopardstown the following year. This put him bang into the Grand National picture and Mr Rank must have held the highest hopes for him, along with Tom Dreaper. It was not to be. J.V. Rank died in January and on 5 April 1952, running under the banner of Mr Rank's executors and with Pat Taaffe in the saddle, *Early Mist* was one of ten runners to fall at the first fence.

Two months later, at the Rank dispersal sale, *Early Mist* found himself moved from Tom Dreaper's stables to those of one Vincent O'Brien in County Tipperary, sold to new owner Mr Joe Griffin for a price of 5,300 guineas. A post-War millionaire, 'Mincemeat Joe' was to rocket into racing, win a huge sum of money, and lose even more, going out of the game bankrupt a few short years after entering it – yet in that time he had owned two Grand National winners.

Few, if any, on the Turf either before or since the reign of Vincent O'Brien can match his quiet, meticulous genius. Those who might attempt to under one code cannot under the other and vice versa. Before he became perhaps the most famous of all flat trainers Vincent was breaking records under NH Rules. Horses trained by O'Brien won the Grand National in three consecutive years: *Early Mist* in 1953, *Royal Tan* in '54 and *Quare Times* in '55.

Not only has he left his mark on the training of racehorses – many younger trainers today state he was a great influence on them – but he also influenced the direction of horseracing as a business, modernising it to a degree that would have been unrecognisable at the time of his birth in 1917.

Growing up hunting and point-to-pointing close to the venue of the first ever steeple-chase (which ran from Buttevant to Doneraile, County Cork, in 1752) Vincent nearly became a butcher, for he knew he was too far down the family pecking order to inherit enough land on which he could train.

Luckily he had shown enough hint of his genius on the point-to-point circuit for a few people to support him. When his training career did begin it was modest – but clever. He bought a horse from the Newmarket Sales during World War II for 130 guineas and acquired a couple of patient owners. By the end of his very first season he had achieved success in both the Irish Cambridgeshire, at the Curragh, and Cesarewitch at Newmarket Racecourse.

His secret lay in planning ahead, in patience, and in meticulous attention to detail. Horses, their welfare and their well being, came first in his life. Between 1948 and 1955 O'Brien-trained horses won the Cheltenham Gold Cup four times (*Cottage Rake*, three times, and *Knock Hard*, once); the Grand National three times (*Early Mist*, *Royal Tan* and *Quare Times*); the Champion Hurdle three times (*Hattons Grace*); and an Irish Grand National (*Alberoni*).

Then he was out of it, away into the bigger business of flat racing and literally minting a fortune, always through hard

work, high intelligence and attention to detail. Betting was a big part of his life; to begin with a necessity, from which he earned enough to expand, and later, one suspects, for the joy of it, that love affair with the bookies that so many punters enjoy.

While Mr Rank spent a sporting lifetime trying to win the Grand National, Joe Griffin burst in expensively, expansively, and won two Nationals in a row, won more than 100k in two bets on *Early Mist*, lost half that amount betting later that year, and before 1954 was out was bankrupt, and out of the game again. His brief sojourn into racehorse owning had twice netted him what others spend a lifetime trying to achieve, Grand National wins with *Early Mist* and *Royal Tan.*

◆ ◆ ◆

The two horses met in the 1952 Grand National, the one in which *Early Mist*, at that time still trained by Tom Dreaper, fell at the first, along with nine others. *Royal Tan*, on the other hand, ran a superb race and looked certain to win until he fell at the last fence. It was almost a carbon copy of his run in 1951 when, poised to win, a last fence blunder left jockey Phonsie O'Brien, Vincent's brother, literally picking him up off the ground, miraculously still in the saddle. But his winning opportunity was gone, and the pair finished second to *Nickel Coin*, the last mare to win the race.

Royal Tan then suffered leg trouble and missed the 1953 season.

Joe Griffin, meanwhile, had also purchased *Early Mist* and so he became his first National winner. He was ridden by Bryan Marshall whose advice to young jockeys riding Aintree for the first time was, 'let down your jerks [i.e. lengthen the stirrup leathers], go round the inside and take your time.'

The 1952 Cheltenham Gold Cup winner, *Mont Tremblant*, was top weight and ran a gallant race to finish second, but it was *Early Mist*, ridden in copybook style, who overcame his first fence fall of the previous year to run out a twenty-length winner – but not until he, too, had survived a monumental mistake at the last fence. A picture shows Bryan Marshall having slipped his reins (let them run through his fingers increasing their length) and shot his lower legs forward, so that his legs make a parallel line with his arms and reins, so giving the horse every chance to balance himself when landing awkwardly and, in particular, to help the jockey retain his seat. Had he been leaning forward with legs back, in show-jumping style, he would have been pitched over the horse's head and unseated.

Like *Caughoo* six years before him, *Early Mist* was given a tremendous reception at home. Three hundred of Joe Griffin's employees and a band greeted the hero as he disembarked from the ferry, and then paraded down O'Connell Street flanked by the owner's lorries decked in streamers in his colours of red, blue and yellow, ending with a reception by the Lord Mayor in the Mansion House. Back home in Cashel, the famous rock was lit up with bonfires, the houses bore bunting in the owner's colours, and free beer flowed. The triumphant party were greeted with rousing cheers and more bands.

It was an incredible year for Vincent O'Brien, even by his standards, for he won the Gold Cup with *Knock Hard*, the Grand National with *Early Mist* and, to his great credit, the Irish Derby with *Chamier*, the first of forty-three English and Irish Classic wins in his illustrious career.

Early Mist did not run in the 1954 National, but was to try twice more in '55, finishing ninth, and '56 when he fell at the first fence.

◆ ◆ ◆

Royal Tan was another strapping chestnut, darker in colour than his stable companion and with a distinctive broad white blaze. By *Tartan*, he was bred near to Vincent O'Brien's, at Tullamaine in County Tipperary by Mr J. Toppin; he was fourth in a hurdle at four years

for Mr P. Bell in 1948, and was bought the following year by Mrs Moya Keogh, to join her
great duo *Hatton's Grace* and *Knock Hard*. Today their son Michael Keogh keeps a few
horses in training and describes a picture of himself at six years old sitting on *Royal Tan*.
His father, Harry, was a Dublin businessman and he remembers his parents as 'well-known
and lucky owners'. Michael was drawn to farming and horses, spending a couple of educative
years as assistant trainer to Vincent, and he is still close to the O'Brien family.

Royal Tan was soon off the mark, winning a novice chase at Leopardstown in 1950. The
following year he was second in the Irish Grand National, second in the Grand National
and won a hurdle at Cheltenham, at which point Joe Griffin entered the fray. Whether or
not the Keogh's wanted to sell is conjecture, but one can only imagine his cheque book
must have been open-ended to prise such a horse away from owners with the stature of
Harry and Moya Keogh.

He was to run in five Grand Nationals, looking the likely winner in his first two but for
last fence errors, missing a year through leg trouble, and then returning to fulfil his high original promise in 1954. He had to do it the hard way in what turned out to be a thrilling race.

Only twenty-nine went to post in 1954, but there was no shortage of spills and thrills
(and the tragic loss of four horses, too.) Both the first and second fences saw departures
and by the time the first Becher's was reached (fence six) a total of nine had already fallen.

Bryan Marshall was a great horseman and he rode *Royal Tan* beautifully, being 'well off
the pace' on the first circuit before taking closer order and then going into the lead at the
last Valentines with only *Tudor Line* appearing to be a serious challenger. Coming up the
long run-in, *Tudor Line* looked beaten but then, much to his credit and the skill of jockey
George Slack, he managed to get going again, gaining with every stride so that they were
only beaten a neck on the line.

For a horse that had had a 'leg' *Royal Tan* showed remarkable soundness, not just in this
race, but also in finishing twelfth in 1955 under a heavy weight burden, and then a gallant
third in 1956. He was by this time owned by Prince Aly Khan who had bought him at Joe
Griffin's dispersal sale following the former owner's bankruptcy. This was his third owner
in his chasing career, but he was fortunate in remaining with one trainer, Vincent O'Brien,
throughout.

◆ ◆ ◆

Jimmy the postman was whistling as he did his rounds of Gaybrook, a tiny village near
Mullingar, County Westmeath, on the morning of March 26, 1955. He climbed through a

hedge to cut a mile off one route, he 'power walked' up the avenue to a big house, he cut back to the row of farm workers' cottages. There, on the doorstep of one, stood a woman, arms akimbo, and she looked prepared for a chat.

'What do you reckon for the National today, then, Missus? Have you thought about the local horse?' he asks.

'Na, not a hope! Such a horse wouldn't stand a chance against the might of all those English horses. I'm not bettin' on him.'

'You could be wrong there', says Jimmy, 'the Grand National is any man's race and my money is on *Quare Times*.'

Posterity does not record whether the woman – or even Jimmy, for that matter – was among the throng to line the main street through Mullingar all the way from Dublin Bridge to Green Bridge to welcome home the hero a few days later.

That *Quare Times* was Vincent O'Brien's third consecutive winner of the great race, with three different horses, is possibly the greatest testament of all to his training. A big, well-bred bay gelding by *Artist's Son* with undoubted ability, he was nevertheless a difficult horse to keep sound, and only a month before the event Vincent had to steer an unexpected journalist away from his stable where he was nursing, this time, a bruised foot. The past had seen dodgy knees, and 'leg problems' which is usually a euphemism for strained tendons.

Phil Sweeney bred *Quare Times* at his Orwell Stud near Thurles, County Tipperary; he named him after a local greyhound. The youngster was consigned to Ballsbridge Sales, Dublin, as a yearling in 1947 where he was sold for 300 guineas. The purchaser was Major Robert Smyth who gave him as a wedding anniversary gift to his wife, Cecily. She turned out the gawky youngster on her husband's estate at Gaybrook, County Westmeath, for him to fill out and grow and mature.

Gaybrook House is no more, having been pulled down and the approximately 1,000-acre estate divided into about sixty smaller farms by the Land Commission in the 1970s. Today one can see the remains of a huge stone building, complete with upper storey windows, that had been a farm building; there is no trace of the butcher's shop that once went with it. Across the road are the remains of the stable yard, but no sign of what was once an orchard. Some of the fields are still divided by stone walls.

Cecily was a colourful character, especially in the hunting field. Born Cecily Mildred O'Carroll Darby of Leap Castle, County Offaly, Cis, as she was known, first married Anthony Minchin of Doorly Hall, County Longford. Theirs was by all accounts a lively marriage, and one day while out with the Westmeath Hunt she took her hunting crop to him. That was it, off he went.

Into her life came Major Robert Smyth of Gaybrook who liked a bit of spirit; he divorced his first wife, who was perhaps a bit too spirited, to marry Cis in 1935, by now also divorced. While waiting for his divorce to come through he moved to Scotland where a dependable nanny, Derry Wilkinson, looked after the daughter of his first marriage, while his son, now Sir Richard Nugent, was sent to live with the Barton family in Straffan House, (now the K Club), County Kildare. Cis suspected Robert Smyth of having an affair with the nanny and sacked her. Major Smyth died three years before *Quare Times*' National and Cis brought a new husband, Bill Welman, into Gaybrook.

Remarriage lost Cis inheritance rights to Gaybrook, although she was allowed to rent it. It was sold in the 1950s, and in the 1970s it was acquired by the Land Commission, fell into disrepair, and finally was demolished.

Bill and Cis Welman moved to Ballymore Eustace, County Kildare. *Quare Times* retired there with them, and after his death at a venerable twenty-eight years old was buried on the front lawn.

By the time *Quare Times* was five he was still too immature to run, and Vincent O'Brien warned the owner it was likely to be 'a long, long time' before he would be ready.

He finally reached a racecourse at six, but precious little promise was shown in three runs for he ran unplaced in a flat race, in an amateur riders' maiden hurdle, and in a novice steeplechase. Injury then saw him side-lined for just over a year, but this may have been a blessing in disguise, for the big bay finally grew into himself.

In January 1954 he won a 2½-mile novices chase in Gowran and then was brought down in Leopardstown. He had been going so well in that race, however, that he was made a hot favourite for Cheltenham's four-mile National Hunt Chase, a race Vincent had predicted ten months earlier that he would win. With top amateur Bunny Cox in the saddle he gave a flawless exhibition to beat his twenty-five rivals, and to land a nice touch for the stable.

It also brought him into the 1955 Grand National picture; although Vincent warned he would not want heavy ground. He had four runners, his previous two winners *Royal Tan*, to be ridden by Dave Dick, and *Early Mist* (Bryan Marshall), along with *Quare Times* (Pat Taaffe) and *Oriental Way* (Fred Winter). The night before the race, after two days of incessant rain, Vincent brought his four jockeys together and showed them past films of the race. He gave them all his usual instructions,

'Keep out of trouble on the outside for the first part of the race and then make steady headway'.

On the morning of the race it was still pouring with rain and that was the way it stayed. Water was lying in pools on the course and racing was nearly called off. In the end, for the first time in its history, the water jump was dolled off. It was still raining as the thirty horses and riders circled at the start, eager to be off, but held up for six minutes by a horse appropriately called *Wild Wisdom* who was playing up.

Among the spectators were Pat Taaffe's parents and his fiancée, Molly Lyons. Pat's father, Tom, also had a runner in the race, the not un-fancied *Carey's Cottage*, ridden by Pat's younger brother, Tos (Thomas). In all, eight horses had travelled over from Ireland, including the race favourite, *Copp*, ridden by Tim Molony for trainer Paddy Sleator; all of them featured in the top thirteen of the betting.

Although Vincent had feared heavy ground for *Quare Times*, the big horse and Pat Taaffe, riding very short for the era (that is, with a short stirrup length), set up an immediate rapport, popping the fences fluently and sploshing through the ground; it is often easier when it is that wet than when the surface water has gone, leaving thick, gluey mud. He made a mistake at the first Valentines while at the Canal Turn *Carey's Cottage*, ridden by Tos, had his nose on the ground, that's how close he was to falling.

Heading out on the final circuit the remaining field was headed by *Sundew*; the big chestnut had led almost from flag-fall, but now, riding to orders perfectly, Pat Taaffe brought *Quare Times* on to the scene, and by the Canal Turn he showed in front. His brother, Tos, showed momentarily in front at the last ditch on *Carey's Cottage*, and here the tiring *Sundew* unseated his rider. His turn was to come two years later when scoring under Fred Winter. To an excited Taaffe family and hundreds of Irish supporters in the stands it looked for a while as if it could be a Taaffe brothers one-two. Instead, it was Pat's day. *Quare Times*, in spite of the conditions, was still full of running and he saw off the challenge of *Tudor Line* (also second the previous year) and *Carey's Cottage* with ease. *Early Mist* and *Royal Tan*, shouldering 12st 3lbs and 12st 4lbs respectively, could not cope with their weight in the ground and faded to finish ninth and twelfth.

Five of the first six horses home were Irish-bred. It was Pat's fifth ride in the National and he had previously fallen three times and finished fourth. He was to win the race again in 1970 on the English-trained *Gay Trip*, trainer Fred Rimell's third of four winners, after *ESB* and *Nicolaus Silver* and before *Rag Trade*.

The midlands town of Mullingar, which

The
GRAND NATIONAL

THE CHRISTENING OF THE BROOK BY CAPT. BECHER. 1839.

FOR THE FESTIVAL OF BRITAIN

We offer as a key

The GREATEST CHASE in lighter vein

Portrayed in A · B · C

B Stands for BECHER
A rider of fame
Who fell in the BROOK
Which now bears his name

C Stands for CANAL
The jump with a TURN
Before you can take that
A lot you must learn

D Stands for DISTANCE
Well OVER FOUR MILES
With jumps to affright you
Nothing like stiles

E Stands for EARL
There are two who live near
Lords DERBY and SEFTON
Both STEWARDS here

was to lose its own racecourse in 1967, celebrated the victory in style (as it was to do for Michael O'Leary's Cheltenham Gold Cup hero *War of Attrition* in 2006). In 1955 *Quare Times* was brought straight from the ferry to his owner's hometown where they found a fantastic reception awaiting them.

Mullingar Town Commissioners' Chairman Mr D. Keelan and County Manager Mr M.G. McGeeney welcomed Vincent O'Brien, Pat Taaffe, Cis Welman and breeders Mr and Mrs Sweeney. Two bands, the Mullingar Brass and Reed Band and the St Mary's Pipe Band led the parade. *Quare Times* took it all in his stride. The Master of the Westmeath Hunt, Col. Denis Purdon, and other mounted members flanked him as they paraded. The human connections were taken in an open topped jeep past the cheering crowds, all of it filmed by the Newsreel cameras. Then it was on to the Greville Arms Hotel – still the town's traditional venue for various functions – for free refreshments and pats on the back all round.

The evening was not yet over for either *Quare Times* or the revellers. The horse was brought back to Gaybrook for the night where a huge bonfire was lit and celebrations continued long into the night.

Next day, the arduous journey back to Vincent's stables was interrupted with two more parades for *Quare Times*, in Thurles, where he was bred, and Cashel, where he was trained. Just five weeks later, on the eve of Pat Taaffe's wedding, the pair won again, a hurdle race in Leopardstown.

Quare Times' jockey Pat Taaffe – forever to be remembered for his association with *Arkle* – was a born horseman and in 1941, at the age of eleven, was selected by the judges at the RDS annual Horse Show in Ballsbridge, Dublin, as 'the most promising rider in the show.'

Pat began his racing career as an amateur, often riding for Dan Moore as well as for his father, and gained his first win on New Year's Day 1946; two years later he won the Kildare Hunt Cup at Punchestown, and in 1949 he rode his first winner for Tom Dreaper. In 1950 he turned professional and was attached to Tom Dreaper's yard. In the late 1950's he broke in a beautiful horse called *Mill House* who was to feature in the early 1960s as *Arkle's* main rival, when *Mill House* was by then domiciled in England. In the year that he won the Grand National on *Quare Times* Pat also won the Irish Grand National and the Galway Plate, both on a horse called *Umm*. He was on a crest, but next year crashed.

Pat might never have ridden the mighty *Arkle* because a year after his Grand National win on *Quare Times* his career was almost shattered in a hurdle race fall in Kilbeggan. Unconscious for ten days and semi-comatose for several weeks more, he lay in hospital fighting for his life.

He not only survived, but he also became nothing short of a legend. He died in 1992 after heart trouble; his wife, Molly, passed away in 1994. Pat's name remains revered in racing circles today.

10

1958 – MR WHAT

ONE OF THE REASONS PAT TAAFFE was an unassuming man – one who never let fame change him – was his upbringing, the example set by his father, Tom, and mother, Kitty. He would not say much, but when he did, the listener could learn a lot.

In 1910 Pat's father, Tom, had emigrated to Australia, seeking his fortune; he expected to be farming, but found himself mostly breaking in and dealing with horses; it was a tough, lean life. Ten years later he walked back into his parents' shop in Ardee, County Louth, penniless.

In 1925 he married Kitty Nugent of Rathcoole; it was still his intention to be a horse dealer rather than a trainer, but he trained one for himself, a mare named *Southern Lass*. The following year the mare won a chase in Haydock Park, after which a couple of friends asked him to train for him. Tom had had a 'huge gamble' on *Southern Lass*, winning enough to change his life forever. He grew into one of Ireland's most successful trainers though there was one poor season in which his horses notched twenty-three second places; eventually one of them won – and was promptly disqualified. Such is racing life.

Tom and Kitty reared three sons, Bill, Pat and Tos, and a daughter, Olive; they brought them up to be modest, no matter how much they were in the limelight. For their riding, all three boys were coached with skill by their father, first learning to ride, then progressing through show jumping and hunting to point-to-pointing and racing. Bill and Pat both played rugby at school, though Pat broke his wrist when he was thirteen years old. It must have given him a foretaste of racing injuries to come …

Tos also became a professional jockey, but Bill went into business as an accountant. Tos and his wife Anne are still alive and living in Kilcullen.

It was in about 1950 that Tom Taaffe noticed a young horse in a field near Mullingar on his way home from racing in Roscommon. He had an 'eye' for a horse, he just liked him. A five-year-old, the bay was on the small side but was broken and had hunted a few times. Tom bought the horse that was to be called *Mr What* – because nobody could think of a name for him – for £500 from his breeder, Mrs Barbara O'Neill. His choice was testament to his good 'eye', for a number of English trainers had already turned him down.

There had also been a 'hairy' moment when Jimmy Tormey from nearby Bunbrosna had taken him out hunting and got stuck in a bog near Lake Derravaragh; perhaps that's what made him so sure-footed around Aintree! Jimmy also rode him in his first race, finishing mid-division in a bumper in Mullingar. He remembers *Mr What* as 'a lovely, big horse, straightforward and never any trouble.' He also trained *General Symons* who dead-heated for third place in the 1972 Grand National. His father, Edward, bred *Leney Princess*, a great NH mare who spawned a dynasty of top steeplechasers.

Barbara O'Neill (née Malone) moved from Shinglis, County Westmeath, to Rathganny, Multyfarnham, near Mullingar, when she married Arthur O'Neill; she brought with her a thoroughbred mare named *Duchess of Pedulas* that she had inherited from her mother, Catherine Percy Malone, who had originally bought the mare for £18. The mare never raced, but she proved to be a prolific breeder of NH winners including *Mr What*. She also produced a filly called *What A Daisy* who in turn bred a further Grand National winner in *L'Escargot*, as well as *Havago*, who won the Gloucestershire Hurdle, Cheltenham; *What A Buck*, winner of nine chases; *Flitgrove*, three chases; *The Pilgarlic*, seven chases and a regular at Aintree, and other winners.

Maeve Wilson from Carbury, County Kildare, was about eighteen years old when her sister, Clodagh, rang from Ontario, Canada, to advise her to back *Mr What* in the Grand National. Maeve cycled to Edenderry in order to place a shilling on the horse, only her second ever bet. Horses were not much part of her life then, her preference being shooting and fishing. Never could she have guessed then that she would marry the son of the breeder of both *Mr What* and *L'Escargot*.

Her friend Mary was Dick O'Neill's first wife, but sadly she died when in her thirties. Maeve then married Dick, and they had four children to go with the four from his first marriage, the youngest of whom, Clair, now carries on the breeding. Out in the fields nearby now is the thirty-one-year-old retired brood mare, *Baronston*, running out with a nice filly both tracing back to the foundation mare, *Duchess of Pedulas*.

Maeve remembers her mother-in-law, Barbara O'Neill, breeder of two Grand National winners, as, 'very much a daughter of the ascendancy, home educated – and wild as a March hare.

'She was good company, told great stories, loved cats and animals, was a good cook and enjoyed her hunting friends.'

The O'Neill policy was to break the youngsters, educate them in the hunting field, and sell them on, and is still the same today.

Mr What proved a promising young horse. He won a maiden hurdle in Navan, a handicap hurdle in Leopardstown, and a two-mile flat race in Phoenix Park.

Tom Taaffe intended to keep *Mr What* for himself and had him entered in a chase in Navan, along with another runner. A businessman, Mr David Coughlan who had owned *Carey's Cottage*, third in the 1955 National, expressed an interest in buying a jumper and Tom gave him the pick of the two. *Mr What*, who had fallen in his only chase the previous season, unexpectedly won in Navan and so became Mr Coughlan's purchase for £1500.

David 'Tone' Coughlan, born 1898 in Skibbereen, County Cork, emigrated to the US aged eighteen, and returned twenty years later, after a bank in which he had funds went out of business and he lost considerably.

He set up a factory at The Harbour, Bray, County Wicklow, and lived with his wife, Rita O'Riorden, and family in a splendid house at the top of the town; he is remembered by Michael McCann, son of his accountant and company secretary for many years, Norah McCann, as a convivial host, and a benefactor of St Brendan's CBS secondary school where Michael was a pupil.

David Coughlan was a small, dynamic man with salt-and-pepper greying hair, soft spoken with a slight American accent, and was very business-focused.

His firm manufactured dental care products, under licence from the US owners in the

F

Stands for FENCES
So broad, tall and tough
THIRTY they number
You'll find that enough

G

For GRAND NATIONAL
The race with a THRILL
Here Jockey and Gee
Oft' meet with a spill

H

Stands for HORSE
HERO of Chases
Gallant when jumping
And showing his paces

I

INTERNATIONAL
For here you will find
Folk of all Countries
" Sports " of all kind

J

Stands for JOCKEY
Whose COURAGE and SKILL
Take him round AINTREE
With never a spill

K

Stands for KNOWLEDGE
Of what must be done
Before this GREAT RACE
Can ever be run

BELOW: Maeve O'Neill and her daughter Clair with two descendents of Grand National winners Mr What *and* L'Escargot. *Clair's grandmother, Barbara O'Neill, owned the foundation mare,* Duchess of Pedulas.

1950s, then he branched out into the manufacture of copper sulphate fertilisers for farming in an adjoining factory.

Michael recalls,

'Through my late mother working for him, my younger brother and I got summer employment in the factory at the harbour in the late 50s. It was the time when every lad in Bray had a summer job – Bray then being Ireland's answer to Blackpool.'

Mr What (by *Grand Inquisitor*) improved rapidly as his confidence grew. He won more chases in Dundalk, Powerstown Park (Clonmel) and Naas, and was second in the Leopardstown Chase. By now, the eight-year-old was being readied for Aintree.

'Preparation takes months, not weeks and must start before Christmas,' Tom Taaffe explained to a newspaper reporter, 'and plenty of long, steady work to teach him to settle and to husband reserves for that tough 4½-mile slog.'

The fruition of all that work was to come on 29 March 1958 when *Mr What* faced thirty rivals. Neither of the professional Taaffe sons was on him; Tos was riding *Brookling* and Pat

had been booked for another horse, so, a week before the race, Tom Taaffe secured Arthur Freeman for *Mr What*, even though that would mean him carrying 6lbs overweight. Pat's intended mount, meanwhile, had been scratched, but *Mr What* was no longer available, so he took the ride on the Duchess of Westminster's *Sentina*. *Mr What* had beaten *Sentina* in the Troytown Chase in Navan but most pundits considered *Mr What* still too much of a novice for Aintree.

This is where the Aintree factor comes in; *Mr What* thrived on the challenge.

It was fitting that there was to be an Irish winner because the race was sponsored for the first time, and its benefactor was the Irish Hospital Sweepstakes; it also meant that there was to be a five-figure prize for the winner – another first.

Wyndburgh, second to *Sundew* the year before, was favourite with *Goosander* next in the betting, then came five runners on 18-1 including *Mr What* and *Sentina*. *ESB*, lucky winner in 1956 after the collapse on the run-in of *Devon Loch* and now twelve years old, was shouldered with top weight.

None of the thirty-one runners fell at the first, but by the fifth a number had gone and, with *Goosander* and Tim Moloney leading, poor *Mr What* was cannoned into by a loose horse. It hit him so hard that he was knocked sideways and virtually brought to a standstill. Luckily it was early in the race and even more fortunate was that he had a horseman in Arthur Freeman who gave him the time he needed to recover and did not hustle him. It paid off and by the time they were heading out into the country for the last time he had jumped his way into contention. At the second Becher's he popped into the lead and by the Canal Turn he was well clear. He put so many lengths between himself and his remaining rivals from there on that he strolled to a 30-length victory over the mare *Tiberetta* as if he had a feather on his back – not 6lbs overweight in soft ground!

In Skibbereen town, where the owner was born, the bookies were disgorging for nearly a fortnight and bookmakers across Ireland claimed that never in the history of their profession did its members receive such a keelhauling. 'Tone' Coughlan was honoured by a 'gay' reception in Skibbereen. A band met his family party at the outskirts of the town and there was a reception held at the West Cork Hotel.

Bray and its wife had also had a bet on *Mr What* and the bookies lost massively there, too.

The schoolboy Michael McCann was among the winners.

'I put a £1 each way bet on *Mr What* for that race. This was massive money for 1958 and for a young lad. With my well-gotten and well-won gains, I bought a beautiful full-sized second-hand blue BSA bicycle which lasted me for my remaining four years of secondary school.'

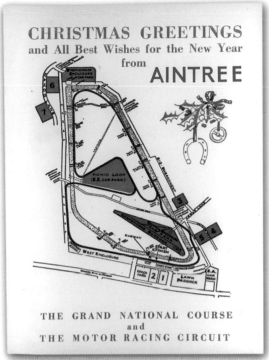

THE GRAND NATIONAL COURSE
and
THE MOTOR RACING CIRCUIT

Two Important Dates
To Remember In
1962

31st March   21st July

The Christening of the Brook by Capt. Bowler, 1839

The International World Championship Motor Race

The Grand National   The R.A.C. British Grand
Steeplechase   PRIX

Interestingly, though, *Mr What*, only eight years old, never won another race, including for trainer Peter Cazalet in England. But he remained an Aintree regular, running in the Grand National six times in all. He was third in 1959, burdened with 11st 9lbs, behind *Oxo* and *Wyndburgh* with *Tiberetta* again the next after him; he fell at the second Becher's in 1960 carrying top weight of 11.11; he was eleventh in 1961 in the race won by *Nicolaus Silver*, carrying 11.9, and it was only in 1962, when he had dropped a full stone in the weights, that he came third again, this time to *Kilmore* and the indefatigable *Wyndburgh*. In his last run he refused the eleventh fence; he was thirteen years old and started at 66-1, ridden by Tommy Carberry, in the race won by *Ayala*.

For several years *Mr What* had to carry big weights, yet in 1958 victory would surely have been his no matter what weight he was carrying, such was the authority of his win.

1975 – L'ESCARGOT

L'ESCARGOT'S STORY IS MUCH MORE than just about the horse, champion though he was. And more than about an owner with a long held dream, gentleman though Raymond Guest, American Ambassador to Ireland, was. It was also the story of two Irish racing families, inextricably entwined.

Dan Moore, a former champion NH jockey turned trainer and his wife, Joan, ran a racing business of high repute based firstly at Fairyhouse and later at Ballysax on the Curragh. They employed an apprentice who not only went on to win the Grand National on *L'Escargot* and become a champion jockey himself, but who also married their daughter, Pamela, and began a whole new generation of racing greats. For after Tommy Carberry married Pamela Moore they had six children, three of whom – Paul, Philip and Nina – are established in the top flight of NH jockeys – and there are more in the wings! Behind every good man (or family), they say, is a woman and Pamela has long been the behind-the-scenes mainstay of the remarkable Carberry family, not only rearing six children, but also playing a full role in the yard, riding out, clipping the horses, encouraging the children and always being a crucial part of the whole operation.

L'Escargot, a chestnut by *Escart III*, was reared like his close relation *Mr What* on the Westmeath pastures, but he was sold as a foal. Seamus Dardis of The Snail Box pub, Ashbourne, County Meath, was buying cattle at the time, but liked the look of the youngster and bought him, reputedly for £725. It was reported that he was going to name him The Snail, but decided that was too derogatory, hence the French equivalent instead.

According to Raymond Guest, in the delightful film, *The Snail, The Diplomat and The Chase*, it was he who chose the name *L'Escargot*. Being by the French horse *Escart III* and half brother to the successful *Havago*, he wanted to create a play on these names and call him 'Let's Go'; that name, however, was not available to register, and so, still playing on the names and the breeding, the dark chestnut became *L'Escargot*. The pub, The Snail Box, still exists at Kilmoon, Ashbourne.

However his name came about, *L'Escargot* was sold on as a two-year-old to Betty Brogan, who died in May 2008, mother of the NH jockey Barry and as a three-year-old he was despatched to Ballsbridge Sales. Enter Raymond Guest, a genial American who achieved his first racing goal of winning the Derby not once, but twice, courtesy of *Larkspur*, 1961, and *Sir Ivor,* 1968, both trained by Vincent O'Brien in County Tipperary. But he nurtured a dream to win the Grand National, too. His first choice in 1957 was *Virginius*, who was brought down at the first fence. His next choice was *Flying Wild*, a fabulous grey mare and one of only a handful of horses ever to beat *Arkle*, though she was admittedly carrying a lot less weight. At Aintree in 1964, quoted joint favourite of four and running in Raymond Guest's chocolate and sky blue hooped colours, she was also a first fence faller. The race was won by twelve-year-old *Team Spirit*, who stood only 15 hands high, on his fifth attempt. Ridden by Willie Robinson, he was bred in County Kildare by Mr. P.J. Coonan and was by top National Hunt sire *Vulgan*. Dan Moore bought him for 250 guineas at Ballsbridge, and from there he was sold to American owners who put him in training with Fulke Walwyn in Lambourn. This race was marred by the fall that saw the paralysis of jockey Paddy Farrell – and was to lead to the founding of the Injured Jockeys Fund.

So Raymond Guest had now had two first fence fallers from two runners, but he was not to be deterred.

As he says in the *The Snail, The Diplomat and The Chase*, the Grand National is extremely hard to win.

Raymond Guest hailed from Virginia and became American Ambassador to Ireland in 1965. After purchasing *L'Escargot*, he placed his striking new acquisition with Dan Moore, one of the most respected men in NH racing.

It was watching the 1928 National that inspired Raymond Guest. His father, Captain

F.E. Guest, had a runner, *Koko*, in it, but he was one of the many to fall or be brought down when the leader, *Easter Hero*, got stuck on top of the Canal Turn. Just two of the forty-two runners remained as *Tipperary Tim* and the American horse *Billy Barton* headed for the last. Naturally, Guest was then rooting for his compatriot but he fell, leaving the race to the Irish-bred horse. In 1931, when a college student, Guest purchased his first horse which never won for him and then, needing the money, he sold it – whereupon it promptly won.

◆◆◆

An expert horseman and brilliant jockey, Dan Moore was described as, 'retiring in disposition, undemonstrative in victory or defeat, and a fair and fearless rider … an outstanding example to young members of his profession.'

One of the owners Dan rode for was the redoubtable Dorothy Paget, about whom bizarre stories have often been recounted. It is said, for instance, that she would think nothing of ringing her trainers in the middle of the night, and would sack them at whim; it is also said that she would demand her staff to bring her a meal in the early hours. And dress sense was anathema to her.

Dan won the Lancashire Chase at Manchester and the Galway Plate, both on *Golden Jack*, for her. He himself found her amusing with a fund of stories.

Dan may be best remembered for a race he did not win. In 1938, riding *Royal Danieli*, before the advent of the photo finish camera, he was beaten by a head in the Grand National by *Battleship* though, as the two horses were wide apart as they passed the post, there were inevitably those who considered the wrong result was called. It was a thrilling race in which neither deserved to lose. *Royal Danieli* had been well hyped in the Press beforehand, following an all-the-way win in Baldoyle, and he ran a blinder in the National. So did the tiny American full horse, *Battleship*, and he went on to be a successful sire in his home country, a life denied almost all NH male horses as the vast majority are gelded (castrated) before they go jumping. *Royal Danieli*, who so nearly added to the Irish roll of honour at Aintree, ran twice more in the race; he fell at the first Becher's the next year and then in *Bogskar*'s 1940 race put in a terrific performance until falling at the second last fence. After

OPPOSITE: *Joan Moore at home with* L'Escargot.

BELOW: *Try, try and try again… patience rewarded at last for* L'Escargot
over his famous rival Red Rum.

that, Aintree was requisitioned by the Army and closed down as a racecourse until 1946.

Dan Moore was born into the world of horses and hunting. His father, T. Levin Moore, was Master of the Ward Union Staghounds, and was followed in that position by Dan's elder brother, Andrew. While Dan was growing up with the Wards, his future wife, Joan Comyn, the youngest of eight children, was hunting with the Galway Blazers, often hacking her pony over to an uncle the night before a meet.

Dan Moore was leading jockey six times and once rode four winners in a day at Cheltenham. He began riding as an amateur and turned professional five years later. Occasionally he rode on the flat, with success, invariably riding a well-judged race. He trained forty-four winners in only his second season in that sphere, and trained successfully for thirty years.

Dan was always an animal lover and Joan recalls that he had a pet fox. One day the Master of the Meath Hunt apologised to him, saying he was afraid the hounds had killed it. Later, Dan whistled, and his fox came to him. Another time, the fox went with him when visiting a friend's house but wary of the strangers, it made a dash for it up their chimney. It was a very sooty Dan and fox who returned home that night.

Joan was herself a fine horsewoman and still cuts a striking figure. After Dan died in

1980, aged nearly seventy, Joan took over the licence and trained about twelve horses. Four years before Dan's death she became the first person in Ireland to install an equine swimming pool, and later an electronic massager for damaged muscles; other trainers came from many miles away to avail of the facility.

The Moores' son, Arthur, was a top amateur rider who won both the Irish Grand National and Ulster National; he began training in 1975, continuing the family tradition with the same sort of modesty and success. Joan herself became manager of Punchestown Racecourse, a role that allowed her to fulfill her natural administrative ability. One of the innovations she introduced was the double bank in front of the grandstands. She wanted

a low profile sponsor for it initially and through Ted Walsh she obtained the ideal person in Betty Moran, American owner of 2000 Grand National victor, *Papillon.* In later years it was renamed Ruby's Double, in honour of Ted's father, and current Irish Champion jockey Ruby Walsh's grandfather.

Dan and Joan's stable jockey was Willie Robinson, forever remembered for his later association with *Mill House*, and their second jockey was the former dual flat apprentice champion Tommy Carberry. It is one thing to be top of the junior flat tree, another to take on seniors over obstacles – and occasionally getting a ride on a 'schoolmaster' or a potentially risky novice. If the ability is there it will come through, barring accidents, but to get a lucky break early in a career and the backing of a trainer is a big bonus.

Dan Moore gave Tommy chances, including a ride in the Cheltenham Festival's Gloucestershire Hurdle (now the Supreme Novices) on a horse called *Tripacer,* and it duly won, a huge boost to the young jockey's burgeoning career. Later when Willie Robinson became stable jockey to Fulke Walwyn in Lambourn, rather than bring in an established jockey, Dan Moore offered the role to Tommy Carberry, who was just twenty years old; he was also to become their son-in-law when he married their daughter, Pamela.

When *L'Escargot* came into training he showed class and ability from the start. Groom, work rider and jockey Mick Ennis, a man who was almost part of the Moore family from the 1950s, looked after him. Mick Ennis went to school in Ratoath, County Meath where he taught a current National buff, one Jim Flanagan, how to play poker. Mick used to 'strap' (groom in a massaging way) *L'Escargot* until his coat shone and his muscles rippled. He was more than Dan Moore's right-hand man, for when he was in his forties he rode the winner of the Ulster National for Dan's son, Arthur, riding *Champerty* to victory in a photo-finish in 1980. He won a number of races, but his reputation was mainly as a 'schooling' jockey, one to ride youngsters sympathetically so that they enjoyed their introductions to racing, leaving the finished article for other jockeys to continue with. Of his equine charges he said,

'They're like well trained babies, they like routine. For a race they have to be right, on the right day, and then hope everything goes right.'

Mick Ennis died in February 2005.

L'Escargot himself won his bumper and his first hurdle race after which he was entered for the National Hunt Festival at Cheltenham in the Gloucestershire (Supreme Novices) Hurdle. When he won this, too, connections knew they had a high-class horse in the making.

A very sound horse, Raymond Guest accurately described him as possessing 'legs like iron, with a wonderful constitution and disposition. He had a short back, powerful hind-quarters, not a beauty of a head – but they don't run with the head, you know!'

L'Escargot was to go on to prove that he was indeed one of the best steeplechasers of either Britain or Ireland by winning two consecutive Cheltenham Gold Cups in 1970-71 – and he also won the prestigious Meadowbrook Chase at Belmont Park in America by a head. So not only did Raymond Guest see him win on his home soil, but he also enjoyed the great honour of him being voted Jumper of the Year in the USA.

They were heady days, but with increasing age came a certain canniness from the horse, so that it was not certain he was always 'putting it all in' (trying hard enough to show his true ability). Inevitably he was also top of the handicap. He went four years without winning another race, and that was the National itself, at no less than his fourth attempt.

He was the sort of horse who, if things went right for him, could rise to the challenge of Aintree. At his first attempt in 1972, they went wrong. He took an instant dislike to the place and was doing his best to stop when, at only the third fence, he was knocked over by another horse.

The next year, despite a run over the fences at Aintree's November meeting, Tommy Carberry famously quoted he 'didn't think [he] would get down to Becher's even in a horsebox!'

But *L'Escargot* was just the sort of horse to surprise. He 'jumped like a buck' and finished an honourable third, giving 23lbs to the winner, a certain horse called *Red Rum*. It was one of

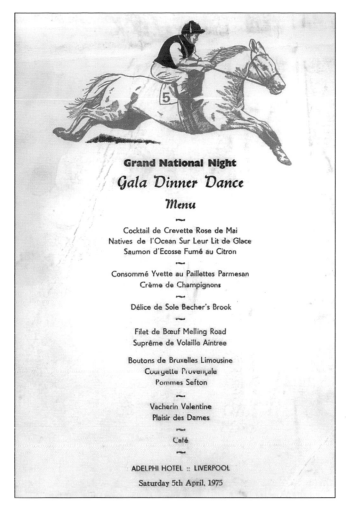

Grand National Night

Gala Dinner Dance

Menu

—

Cocktail de Crevette Rose de Mai
Natives de l'Ocean Sur Leur Lit de Glace
Saumon d'Ecosse Fumé au Citron

Consommé Yvette au Paillettes Parmesan
Crème de Champignons

Délice de Sole Becher's Brook

Filet de Bœuf Melling Road
Suprême de Volaille Aintree

Boutons de Bruxelles Limousine
Courgette Provençale
Pommes Sefton

—

Vacherin Valentine
Plaisir des Dames

—

Café

—

ADELPHI HOTEL :: LIVERPOOL
Saturday 5th April, 1975

the greatest Grand Nationals, with the wonderful Australian horse *Crisp*, joint-top weight with *L'Escargot* on 12 stone, galloping his heart out, treating the big fences like upturned hairbrushes. He was almost 'out for the count' when *Red Rum,* on 10st 5lb, caught him just before the winning post. The next highest weight, *Spanish Steps*, on 11st 3lb, came in fourth.

In 1974 *Red Rum* himself had to carry 12 stone, while *L'Escargot* had come down a pound to 11.13 – and had been trained specifically with the National in mind. But this was the year when *Red Rum*, bred in County Kilkenny by the McEnery family, truly proved himself to be great. He simply skipped round and nothing, neither the weight nor any other horse, was going to deny him. He franked that a few weeks later by also winning the Scottish National.

Tommy summed him up succinctly in Carberry style:

'He went round Aintree like a rabbit – you couldn't knock him down if you tied his legs together. An Aintree horse needs five legs – *Red Rum* had nine!'

By 1975 *L'Escargot* was twelve years old and the stable pet; still without a win since his second Gold Cup victory of 1971, his weight had gone down to a more manageable 11st 3lb. He was also equipped with a pair of blinkers for the National to 'aid his concentration' and focus his mind on the job ahead and not let it wander. He was also given an occasional change of scene by visiting Portmarnock beach for a canter along the sands, a paddle in the sea, and a roll afterwards. With Dan Moore unwell, Joan supervised much of his preparatory work.

Tommy Carberry recalled,

'I had to tune in to him, he could be a little bit temperamental. You could feel his class, but he had to be enjoying himself … he was the best horse I ever rode.'

£'ESCARGOT!

Ireland's winner canes bookies

By JOHN MOORE

THE BOOKIES took a hammering yesterday as L'Escargot—the Snail—thundered home to win the Grand National, the first Irish victory since Mr. What 17 years ago.

His 15-length triumph over hat-trick seeking Red Rum completed a remarkable record for the 12-year-old gelding, who has already won two Cheltenham Gold Cups.

Wonderful

And jockey Tommy Carberry, son-in-law of winning trainer Dan Moore, was also celebrating a unique treble, having won the Cheltenham Gold Cup and the Irish Grand National already this year.

But if Irish punters, and American owner Raymond Guest were cockahoop, their bookies were counting the cost. Terry Rogers, one of Ireland's biggest, said: "We're still counting our losses."

Millionaire Guest afterwards presented _____ horse to his train_____

"H_____

Mr. Guest. "He's proved he's wonderful, and now he's going out to grass.

"We've been trying to win a National for 20 years, and now I'm getting out of racing, too."

It was certainly L'Escargot's turn to win—he was third to Red Rum in 1973, and second to him last year.

Sentimental money made Red Rum 7-2 favourite, with L'Escargot second best at 13-2.

But carpet manufacturer Brian Buckley, 35, who recently shared a meal of snails with England Soccer captain Alan Ball, won £12,500 with an ante-post bet at 20-1. Selwyn Demmy, of Manchester, laid the bet—and paid ___ on yesterday's victor.

L'Escargot being led in after his triumph.

SUPER SNAIL!

L'Escargot turns Grand National tables on Red Rum

L'ESCARGOT — it's French for snail—romped home to a super Grand National victory at Aintree yesterday.

The brilliant Irish chaser had 15 lengths to spare over Red Rum, the hot favourite chasing his third National victory on the trot.

And it was sweet revenge for L'Escargot, who was third in 1973 and

● Just Grov__ ____ ___ ___Escargot and To___ ___

Red Rum, again on 12 stone, was favourite for the race and the punters would think of nothing else.

Raymond Guest brought his wife, Caroline, to Aintree for *L'Escargot's* final tilt at National glory; she had been with him for both his Derby winners – maybe she would bring luck to her nervous husband, who simply admitted to enquirers yet again that 'the National is very hard to win.'

Tommy Carberry, now thirty-three years old, knew exactly how to ride him and was confident of a big run. He carried a lucky snail shell in his breeches pocket.

Before the race he said,

'I think he will run very well; he must be settled or he will run too freely. He's very intelligent which he has to be, and he's careful.'

It was a partnership that could so nearly have ended on the ground; after Becher's first time, at the seventh fence known as Foinavon's, *L'Escargot* made a mistake that catapulted Tommy on to his neck; the horse's head was low to the ground and Tommy perched precariously for a stride; the pair made a great recovery. Fifteen of the thirty-one runners failed to reach halfway.

On the second circuit the leader, *High Ken*, fell at the fence before Becher's leaving the principals as *The Dikler, Spanish Steps, Southern Quest* and last year's winner and runner-up. *L'Escargot* and his pilot cleverly cut the corner at the Canal Turn to save precious lengths; the horse was clearly loving it. The pace was a fast one, but these two began to draw clear of the rest and to those with good binoculars one thing was becoming clear as they crossed the Melling Road for the final time and headed for home: although *Red Rum* and *L'Escargot* were running together, Tommy was actually taking a pull on *L'Escargot*. By the last fence, Brian Fletcher could be seen at work on *Rummy* while Tommy had not yet moved on Raymond Guest's horse. Once he did so, with the last fence safely flicked under him, all he had to do was let the reins out a notch and *L'Escargot* stormed away in the manner of his younger Gold Cup days. In the winner's enclosure Arthur Moore placed his trilby between the victor's ears, and this has become his trademark for big wins.

He thoroughly deserved the victory, while *Rummy*, second again the next year to *Rag Trade*, was to write his name into the record books in 1977 when, as a twelve-year-old, he won for an unparalleled third time.

For his part, Raymond Guest, achieving his life's ambition, made an emotional speech in the Aintree winner's enclosure, saying,

'Immediately I want the world to know I am deeply grateful to my trainer Dan Moore and my jockey, Tommy Carberry.'

Having reached this pinnacle – and joined only the Prince of Wales later King Edward

VII in owning two Derby winners and one of the Grand National – Raymond Guest retired from racing.

Tommy himself had become the only jockey to ride in the same season the winners of The Cheltenham Gold Cup (*Ten Up*), the Irish Grand National (*Brown Lad*), and the Grand National. The day after the Irish Grand National and four days before the Grand National at Aintree Tommy took a fall in which it was feared he had broken his collar-bone; x-rays gave him the all clear but even so he must have still felt bruised two days later when he won the Topham Trophy over the big fences on *Our Greenwood*. His glorious week was crowned with his triumph in the Grand National – and memorable five-course dinner and celebrations in the Adelphi Hotel, Liverpool.

On *L'Escargot*'s return to the Curragh he was, according to Joan Moore, 'mobbed like a film star.'

12

1999 – BOBBYJO

TOMMY CARBERRY ALMOST DID NOT JOIN the racing ranks at all, and nearly became a priest. For all his infectious banter and bonhomie, he is serious at heart. He lost his father, Tim, at a tender, impressionable age in harrowing circumstances, the then thirteen-year-old watching his father die, slowly, from tuberculosis at the age of forty-five. The young Tommy considered joining the priesthood, and even had the necessary papers signed.

It was to racing's gain that the man who was to become champion jockey five times, to win three Cheltenham Gold Cups, and to both ride and train Grand National winners, changed his mind.

Tommy Carberry is one of those indefatigable people who laughs a lot and sees the bright side of situations. He had more than his fair share of injuries in his twenty-one-year riding career, but dismisses them as having 'stayed in one piece.' Cobbled together might be an alternative description for the four broken legs, seven broken collarbones, a broken hip and some broken vertebrae, that he has recovered from.

Tommy's first ride in the Grand National was on *Mr What*, by then thirteen; he uncharacteristically refused at the eleventh fence and Tommy found himself 'face down in the ditch at Valentines, where there were two loose horses trotting up and down.'

In childhood he was accustomed to hard work, especially after his father died, but at school he was the frolicsome, extrovert 'divil'. That could still well describe him; to say nothing of his eldest son, Paul, a riding genius with limpet-like qualities and balance beyond imagination.

The first animal Tommy ever rode was a bullock – put him in a rodeo today and he would do better than most cowboys – and from that moment on he wanted to ride.

Near to his home he would see Dan Moore's string out on exercise. His imagination was fired. Eventually the young lad, weighing barely six stone, plucked up courage to ask for a job.

No-one guessed it then, but Tommy Carberry was on his way. In later years one newspaper reporter described him as having 'good manners, hard work and sometimes outrageous play.' The same has probably been written of his son, Paul.

Inevitably, the lightweight Tommy's prospects were limited at Dan Moore's and so he found himself apprenticed to flat trainer Johnny Lenehan, for a weekly wage of 2/6d.

As an apprentice, life is likely to consist of mucking out stables, riding out, running errands – and dreaming of riding winners, or even of being given race rides at all.

Tommy was given his first ever race-ride on the flat at Naas, but it turned into a nightmare: he was caught up in the starting tapes and nearly hung. Eventually, after disentangling himself, he trailed in last, his face covered in blood. He feared his first ride was also going to be his last.

Before long, he won on a horse named *Ben Beogh* on the Curragh and nineteen further wins followed that season. The following year saw twenty-one wins, and just beaten in a blanket finish in his first Classic ride for the Irish 1000 Guineas. But weight, that perennial problem, began to gain, and so it was that Tommy switched from flat apprentice, albeit a champion one, to steeplechase jockey. He returned to Dan Moore.

The day Tommy won the Gloucestershire Hurdle on *Tripacer* at the Cheltenham NH Festival in 1962 remains as fresh in his memory today as it did then. He followed this up by winning the Galway Hurdle. Cheltenham was to be the scene of thirteen wins for Tommy.

After that first Cheltenham win, lady luck smiled on Tommy again. Dan Moore's faith in the young man was fully justified, none more so than when he 'stole' the 1964 Massey

Ferguson Gold Cup at Cheltenham on *Flying Wild*. *Arkle* was burdened with 12st 10lbs, the grey mare was on 10st 6lb.

Tommy Carberry's first ride at Cheltenham had produced a winner, and so did his last, *Brockshee*, in the 1982 Arkle Chase, trained by his brother-in-law, Arthur Moore.

To him, the injuries he suffered in his career were the 'minutiae' of his trade. His view on injuries was this,

'Steeplechasing is a rare game and has its worries but not of injury; it's more the worry of what rides I'm going to get, or what winners; if you worry about injuries you shouldn't be doing it and if you're happy with what you're doing you are not going to call it dangerous.'

It was ironic that the fall that finished his riding career happened in a flat race. Falls on the flat are comparatively rare, but when they do occur the speed is faster and so the outcome can be serious. When the two-year-old Tommy was riding at Tralee fell, the jockey broke several ribs causing a lung to collapse and leaving him literally hanging on to life by a thread. He was on a respirator for a week, but he recovered in time to want to ride again, a hope firmly dashed by his doctor. Instead he bounced back to carve out a training career for himself, including the 1999 Grand National with *Bobbyjo*.

Tommy's first win as a trainer was with *Royal Appointment* in a Navan novice chase. His has always been a small, family-run stable, on about fifty acres at Ballybin, near the village of Ratoath in County Meath. It normally stables about eighteen horses and all six children play their part, when able to, in its running, while the lynch pin is Pamela herself.

It is to the credit of the whole family that Tommy joined the select, elite band to both ride and train a Grand National winner. It had only been achieved previously by Algy Anthony (*Ambush II* and *Troytown*), Fulke Walwyn (*Reynoldstown* and *Team Spirit*), and twice for Fred Winter, riding *Sundew* and *Kilmore* and training *Jay Trump* and *Anglo*; no-one has done it since.

London publican Bobby Burke was enjoying a drink in a Galway city pub while on a visit to his home-place near Mountbellew one day in 1990. He started chatting to his neighbour, as men in pubs do. The other man, Liam Skehan, told him he bred a few horses, but he was getting into the building trade; as a result he was selling a number of horses.

Drinks and chat flowed, and by the end of the evening Bobby had agreed to buy six of Liam's stock. The batch included a bay foal by *Bustineto*, and Bobby named it after himself and his wife, Jo. The stallion *Bustineto* stood near Thurles but died in 1997. By *Bustino*, he was a 7 furlong horse out of a speedy *Habitat* mare so stamina was not expected to be his forte, let alone that he should produce a Grand National winner.

Bobby Burke gave up betting and sold all but three of his pubs; one of the remaining ones, at Dalston near Carlisle, was renamed the Bobbyjo.

Five years after buying the foal sight unseen (along with the other five) he put the by now handsome gelding into training with Tommy Carberry, a man he admired from having watched him many times as a jockey. From the start, *Bobbyjo* was easy to do and to ride; there was neither a mischievous nor a naughty side to him. He was the same in his races.

Paul Carberry recalled,

'He was very easy to ride, he would settle for you and you could do anything you wanted with him.'

To begin with *Bobbyjo* looked very ordinary; he ran five times without getting anywhere near to placing, let alone winning. Two seconds and a third followed before finally,

in his second season and on his tenth attempt, he won a race, a handicap hurdle off a low weight at Down Royal. Shortly after this, Tommy Carberry himself rode him in a bumper at the Punchestown Festival, finishing third of twenty-six.

The following season, 1996-7, *Bobbyjo* began chasing and immediately his career improved, winning chases at Down Royal, Punchestown and Fairyhouse. He was also second at 20-1 in a Grade 1 Chase at Punchestown.

When he won the Grand National trial at Fairyhouse in February 1997, thoughts of the real thing could be harboured. He was eight years old and first there was to be a crack at the Irish Grand National.

Fairyhouse on Easter Monday is a must in the Irish racing calendar, and for many of the thousands who flock to the County Meath track only thirteen miles from Dublin city on that day, it is their only day's racing of the year. Not even the Easter Rising of 1916 put a stop to the Irish Grand National.

It was April 13, 1998, and twenty-two runners went to post for the prestigious 3 mile 5 furlong event; *Bobbyjo* won it by half a length from *Papillon*. Anyone with a crystal ball could have correctly foretold these two horses as the next two winners of the Grand National at Aintree.

Bobbyjo, a year older than *Papillon*, was the 1999 winner when *Papillon* did not run in it. The full quota of forty (the maximum number of runners allowed, instigated on safety grounds in 1984) was not reached, with thirty-two going to post. This meant that *Bobbyjo*, allotted only 9 stone in the original long handicap was in no danger of being eliminated. There had been two other changes to Aintree conditions since the last Irish winner in 1975; in 1987 the minimum age was raised to seven, and in 1989 some of the fences were modified, notably the famous ditch at the back of Becher's Brook being filled in. The height of the fence (4ft 10in) and the depth of the drop on landing (6ft 9in) have remained the same, but by filling in the brook and levelling the slope back into it, the fence has become safer for horses who fall; they now cannot slip back into the brook, something that could cause a broken back.

Backed down from 20-1 to tens there was plenty of support for him, following a confidence-boosting win in a Down Royal hurdle race the previous month, partnered by Paul Carberry's younger brother, Philip. Not only that, but he now had perfect ground in his favour; he had struggled to show his Irish National form in a number of chases on heavy ground. Now everything was coming right, though he had never tackled the strange Aintree fences before. Bobby Burke brought coach-loads of his customers from his pubs, and they all had bets.

No less than fifteen runners, almost half the field, were on 10 stone, and eight were out

at 200-1 in the betting – but there is no such thing as a sub-standard National. The previous year's winner *Earth Summit* was trying again and the lovely grey *Suny Bay*, second in both the previous two years, was trying to make it third time lucky. Most unusually a mare, *Fiddling The Facts* was favourite, followed by *Call It A Day* ridden by Richard Dunwoody and *Double Thriller*. Next came Tony McCoy's mount, *Eudipe*, and *Bobbyjo*. On the way to the start *Bobbyjo* was bouncing under his pilot; it was Paul's fifth ride in the race.

Once they were off it was *Blue Charm* who led for much of the way and, putting in the run of his life, he hung on to finish a worthy runner-up. Some of the fancied runners fell by the wayside, but Paul Carberry was hugging the inside and was stealthily moving forward. Another Irish runner, *Merry People*, ran a cracker for Garrett Cotter and owners Karl Casey (a director of Tramore Racecourse), K. McHugh and Mrs M. Dowling; the 200-1 shot stormed into the lead two out, only to knuckle over. Garrett remounted and came home sixteenth of the eighteen finishers. It was *Call It A Day* who led over the last but Paul guided *Bobbyjo* up on his outside and the horse jumped as if he had springs in his heels. Sprouting wings he drew steadily clear for a ten-length victory.

It was the first Irish win since *L'Escargot* in 1975 and more than that, the rider of the winner then was the trainer now, and his own son the jockey. It was only the sixth ever father and son combination, and amazingly the feat was to be repeated the next year with Ted and Ruby Walsh.

Paul Carberry and *Bobbyjo* returned to rapturous applause, the cheers raised to the roof as Paul stretched up from the saddle and grabbed hold of the overhead beam like a gymnast for his unorthodox dismount. The Irish were understandably euphoric that the trophy was at last going back over the water, and the celebrations lasted many days and nights, firstly in Liverpool and then in Ratoath where a thousand welcomed the hero to Ryan's pub.

Bobbyjo was to be presented with a total of sixteen awards from Irish newspapers and radio stations during the months that followed, and Tommy was later to be voted Goff's Irish Race Personality of the Year. The whole thing couldn't have happened to a more deserving family.

For Paul to win the Grand National was literally a life's ambition. He was fourteen months old when his father won and he grew up watching films of the race, collecting memorabilia, and dreaming the dream. Totally inspired, he was determined to win it himself. Second son Paul is the best known both on and off a horse. He has inherited his father's devil may care love of life and he is also one of the best NH jockeys of his era or any other; the way he can remain in the saddle when many others would fall owes much to his love of hunting, and the glue-like ability it has given him.

His younger brother Philip is also near the top of the Irish jockey's tree and can boast an Irish National on *Point Barrow* and the Champion Hurdle at Cheltenham on *Sublimity* among his many successes. Their sister, Nina, is widely recognised as far and away the best lady National Hunt rider there has ever been in either Great Britain or Ireland, and she has every chance of becoming the first female jockey to win the Grand National. A natural athlete, she is a fine horsewoman, has excellent race-craft skill, and doesn't suffer from nerves – she simply loves racing.

There are two younger brothers, Mark, who is a carpenter, and Peterjon. Peterjon was champion pony racer in 2004, but his passion is his off-road bike; speed and danger go hand in hand in this family.

That leaves eldest son, Thomas, formerly in bloodstock shipping, and now head lad to trainer Robbie Osborne. In 2006 he took out an amateur licence and won a point-to-point and finished third in a hunter chase. Then on August 4, 2007, at the age of thirty-four and at the Galway Festival, no less, he rode his first winner on the track!

Paul felt convinced he was on the way to winning another Grand National in the 2002 race, won by *Bindaree*. His mount, *Ad Hoc*, was brought down just four fences from home and was travelling every bit as well as *Bobbyjo* had been at the same stage three years earlier, he said.

'I hadn't yet asked him a question and he was going better than anything else. To say I was disappointed is an understatement, I felt sick.'

Paul was fortunate to be able to take the ride on *Bobbyjo*, or to race at all, for three years earlier, when a passenger in a horrific car accident, he was shot like a bullet out of the sun roof and still bears the scar on the side of his face. He has also had many injuries during his racing career, both on and off the track; he imparts great confidence in his mounts, but when things go wrong it can end in a heavy fall. He remains such a genius in the saddle that for as long as he keeps racing he will always be in demand as a rider.

He may be high-spirited, but he is also thoughtful and kind. In 1997 when he won the Galway Plate the jockeys were donating their riding fees that day to the Shane Broderick appeal after that young jockey became paralysed; in addition to his fee Paul donated his full winning percentage, about £4,000;

'It could have been me gone at the first with a broken back,' he said simply.

Bobbyjo ran in one more National the following year, and finished eleventh. He was being prepared for a third crack at it when, in the Grand National Trial at Fairyhouse in February 2001, he was injured during the race; as a result he had to be retired. Later, complications set in and, aged only eleven years, he had to be put down.

He was buried in the grounds of the Mountbellew home of owner Bobby Burke's parents. Bobby had grown up and been to school from there and it was a fitting tribute to his hero.

Bobby said, 'He gave us some wonderful moments.'

Tommy Carberry commented, 'He was a gentleman of a horse and as he grew and matured he became a fine chaser.'

Paul added, 'He was very genuine and he jumped brilliantly.'

Perhaps the most remarkable statistic about *Bobbyjo* is that he never once fell in his forty-eight-race career.

13

2000 – PAPILLON

IN CONTRAST TO BOBBYJO, *Papillon* began winning on the track from his very first race. In fact it was not until his eighth race that he finished out of the frame (the first four). By then he had won a maiden hurdle and, in only his third run, a novice chase, followed soon after by a Grade 3 chase carrying 11st 13lb, and by a fourth in a Grade 1. So high things were expected and received from *Papillon* from the beginning.

The Walsh family live and train at Kill, County Kildare, opposite Goffs Sales, close to Naas. Ted Walsh, recognised by the Irish public today as part of TV racing's double act with Robert Hall when presenting the major race meetings, was the all-time leading amateur rider on either side of the Irish Sea, riding more than six hundred winners. Today he combines being a successful trainer of a number of top horses with his TV punditry.

He spent a few years as a young child in America when his father, Ruby, followed two of his brothers to the 'promised land'. Ruby left the pub he ran in County Cork, where he also farmed, dealt in horses, provided troop horses, hunted, and rode with success in point-to-points. The American dream did not last long – they found the

winters bitterly cold — but the connection forged with the States was never lost.

On return, Ruby bought a yard in the Phoenix Park and trained and dealt in horses right there in the city centre; Phoenix Park racecourse was still thriving then. In 1960 they moved to their current place in Kill, where Ruby remained training and to a greater extent dealing until his death in 1990. Ted, meanwhile, forged his incredible amateur career, and began training after his father's death. He and his wife, Helen, have since watched their son, also named Ruby, become the youngest champion amateur at seventeen and the youngest professional champion two years later.

In 1995 *Papillon* was bought privately as an unbroken four-year-old after failing to sell in the ring at Doncaster. He came home to Kill and, after breaking, began to show enough promise for Ted to feel confident about selling him to a patron.

Enter the American connection.

A SmithKlein Beecham millionairess Betty Moran of Malvern, Pennsylvania, was a feted bloodstock breeder whose stock was bought and sold for millions of dollars. She owned and bred the Belmont Stakes winner, *Crème Freche*, the Belmont Stakes being the third leg of the American Triple Crown along with the Kentucky Derby and the Preakness Stakes.

Betty first came to know Ruby Walsh senior when her son, Michael, wanted to be a NH jockey and, through an ex-pat mutual friend, he was despatched to the Walshes. An instant rapport was set up between the two families, and although Betty's chief racing interests lay on the flat she kept one or two with Ruby in Ireland. So when Ted suggested she buy the as yet unraced *Papillon* she trusted his judgement and agreed to the purchase. There were a good few times that she flew across the Atlantic to watch him run down the field, she was later to lament.

But she was there for the National; the miracle was that the horse was, for Betty Moran had taken a good deal of persuasion to allow him to be entered, let alone run. She had heard too many rumours of deaths at Aintree to want to risk her horse. *Papillon* was by now nine, had finished second to *Bobbyjo* in the Irish National, had won the Ladbroke Chase at Cheltenham, and had demonstrated a touch of class by having the speed to beat a good two-miler called *Opera House* over that distance. Nevertheless it was now more than a year since he had won anything; the question hovered, was he putting it all in? The challenge of Aintree might just bring out the best in him.

To begin with, Betty Moran remained adamant, until finally a friend persuaded her. Even then, it was only after she had walked the course with Ted Walsh on the eve of the race that she gave the final go-ahead.

Later she recalled thinking, 'This is ridiculous.'

Punters and pundits evidently thought otherwise. After many tips for him, *Papillon*'s price tumbled overnight from 33-1 to start 10-1 second favourite, to Tony McCoy's mount *Dark Stranger*.

Ruby Walsh had missed most of that winter through a horrific leg break sustained in Czechoslovakia and was lucky to be back in the saddle. He gave *Papillon* a copybook ride, avoiding many riderless horses, including *Dark Stranger*, and cruised into a share of the lead with two to jump. A clutch of others was in close

With much appreciation
for all your kind wishes and thoughts
of Papillon
The 2000 Martell Grand National Winner

Ted Walsh

contention and of these it was *Mely Moss* who posed the biggest danger. *Papillon*'s head landed just in front over the last fence and began to draw clear, but his rival pursued him spiritedly, producing a thrilling finish between the two.

The Irish cheers were louder than ever when *Papillon* held on by 1¼ lengths. The country had gone forty years with only one winner, now suddenly it had two in a row. All the more remarkable and praiseworthy was that it was again a father and son combination.

The connections and friends partied long into the night at Kill. Betty Moran had been booked on a flight back home that night. Not a hope. She remained until the Tuesday. And generously called for drinks all round in the pub in Kill.

Talking to a news reporter some five months later she quipped, 'I'd better ring and see if they've stopped serving yet.'

Those who were there will never forget the 2001 running of the Grand National. It survived, just, the foot and mouth epidemic; and then it survived, marginally, the deluge that poured onto the course leaving it the wettest for many a long year. The conditions were difficult and there were a huge number of falls, but the ground was so soft that injuries were minimal. The biggest 'take-out' occurred at the first Canal Turn when a loose horse careered across the front of it, baulking approaching horses so that altogether ten fell or were knocked out of it like a pack of cards. By the end of the first circuit only seven runners remained of the forty that started out, and they had it all ahead of them again when, once more, loose horses caused interference. In the end only *Red Marauder* and *Smarty* stood standing to finish in that order, with the remounted *Blowing Wind* and *Papillon* hacking along steadily to eventually finish third and fourth.

Papillon missed the 2002 season because of a ligament injury. He came back into training for 2003, but the prospect of retirement loomed because he was becoming a bit 'canny'; instead of moving up a gear when needed, he would actually change down when pressure was applied.

Papillon was retired in March 2003, shortly before a further attempt on the Grand National. He had run lethargically in a hurdle race at Punchestown and that told his connections to call 'time'.

Ted Walsh said,

'I made it clear that he would have to show us he was enjoying himself and that he was up to the task of another National. I rang the owner and she agreed it was time for retirement.

'He's been a fantastic horse to be involved with and did us all proud. Winning the National with Ruby riding was a day we will never forget, and we had other good days, too.

'He's retired sound and looking a picture as he always did.'

Today *Papillon* lives out his retirement lazing in the fields around the Walsh home, his

companion being the twenty-nine-year-old *Barney Burnett*. *Barney* was trained by Ted's father; *Barney* is a stout old soul, more so than *Papillon* who doesn't thrive if left out in the winter; so he, at a comparatively youthful eighteen years old, comes in at night while *Barney* remains outdoors.

'When we take his rug off in April, ready for the summer months, *Barney* always looks magnificent,' says Ted.

Betty Moran was a diehard flat-race enthusiast who was quoted as saying she'd rather win a Group 1 at Royal Ascot than watch jumping.

'I'm not a steeplechasing person, it's all trophies and no money.'

Jumpers are mainly geldings running for small purses with nil stud prospects, she surmised: Betty Moran had recently sold a yearling for $2.5million; her *Crème Freche* had won $4million with which she had turned her Brushwood Stables into one of the leading breeding establishments in America.

Nevertheless she had also won steeplechasing's most famous trophy. And when she returned to her priceless bloodstock in America she commissioned a portrait of *Papillon* to hang alongside that of *Crème Freche*.

14

2003 – MONTY'S PASS

THE NICELY-BRED FOUR-YEAR-OLD BAY GELDING looked impressive as he walked round the sales ring and several would-be purchasers were set to bid for him. Then came the bombshell. The auctioneer read out the vet's certificate: 'This gelding has a heart murmur and is not considered suitable for racing.'

Ten years later Jimmy Mangan smiles as he says of his 2003 Grand National winner, 'If ever a horse had the greatest heart it was *Monty's Pass.*'

It is all a part of the inexact science of horse racing and veterinary medicine; a horse with a 'perfect' heart can drop dead without forewarning, one with a heart murmur can lead a full life – and win the world's most challenging horse race.

Ireland has seen phenomenal change to lifestyle during the Celtic Tiger of the 1990s and the booming economy of today, but an enduring Irish country tradition that remains timeless is that of the small time owner/breeder/trainer/dealer of a few thoroughbred horses, often associated with a family farm. Perhaps the most traditional county of all in this respect is Cork.

Drive through Fermoy and on towards Tallow, take a few small turnings, see the River Bride and suddenly there in front of you is a village sign proudly announcing 'Conna – Home of 2003 Grand National Winner *Monty's Pass.*'

Take another small turn or two and you are in Curraheen, the stables of Jimmy Mangan, his wife Mary, twin sons, Patrick and Bryan, and daughter, Jane. Success has brought little change. The set up today is barely altered since Jimmy trained the National winner; he still breeds a little, buys and sells a little, and trains a few more than he did. He will take in the occasional mare to foal for an owner just as his late father, Patrick, did thirty years ago when he foaled *Dawn Run.* No indication then, of course, that the bay filly foal with the long ears would be anything out of the ordinary, let alone the best mare National Hunt racing has ever seen. The foaling was simply a supplement to his income; just as it was for Jimmy when he foaled future Grand National winner *Amberleigh House.*

Jimmy has had several future stars through his hands and regrets not a bit that it is others who have earned from their success; his philosophy is simple:

'I like to see them win when they leave the yard and give people fun.'

Jimmy himself bred *Amble Speedy*, beaten by a short-head, the narrowest margin in the Irish Grand National.

It does his reputation no harm at all to have been the supply source of good horses, though it is amazing to think that he produced the 2002 Grand National winner *Bindaree* as a yearling, readying him for sale, feeding, grooming, and generally preparing him to look his best for the sales ring and then promptly won the race himself the very next year with *Monty's Pass*, in addition to foaling 2004 winner *Amberleigh House* – close connection with three Grand National winners in a row.

'I never thought I would have a runner in the National, let alone win it,' he admits.

Usually, at any one time in his yard, he would have about eight youngsters for sale and about another four to train. Since 2003 the number to train has risen to about twenty,

'But that's where I want to keep it,' he asserts.

There have been some other life changing aspects to training the Grand National winner; he gets recognised wherever he goes in racing; every year he is invited over to the lunch at the Savoy Hotel, London, when the Grand National weights are launched – and he often finds visitors on his doorstep, usually tourists, asking if they can see *Monty's Pass.* The answer, of course, is invariably 'yes'.

Monty's Pass was bred by in County Wexford by Gerry Slattery; he was by *Montelimar* (who also sired *Hedgehunter*) out of a mare by the ultra-game dual Champion Hurdler *Monksfield.* The Slatterys sold him. The purchaser could – should – have expected a decent profit when he resold him as a four-year-old, but then came that shattering veterinary report;

he was lucky to raise IR£4,200. Undaunted, the new owners, the Mobile Syndicate, asked Jimmy to train him and right from the start he showed ability; before long he became something of a course specialist at nearby Cork (Mallow) racecourse.

He did go hunting once, with Mary Mangan, but the venture ended ignominiously with the future Grand National winner getting stuck in a dyke and having to be pulled out.

Most of the inmates at Mangan's are young NH horses starting out on their careers, but *Monty* was one that was left after he won his point-to-points, presumably because of the diagnosed heart problem.

He then took the hunter chase route into chasing and never ran in a bumper; he had been chasing for three years before he ever ran in a hurdle race. His hunter chase tally from

five runs was one win, three seconds and a fourth, ridden in all of them by Davy Nugent.

It was after finishing second to Eddie O'Grady's crack hunter chaser, *Sheltering*, that, out of the blue, Jimmy received a phone call from Northern Ireland. The man at the other end of the line was a stranger to him, Mike Futter, owner of bingo halls throughout Ireland, asking if the horse could be bought.

'I had never spoken to him before,' recalls Jimmy, 'but I told him about the heart murmur – even though he was the healthiest horse in the yard.

'He and his syndicate bought the horse and said they would keep him in training here – it was unreal luck for me.'

The syndicate members with Mike Futter were Adam Armstrong, Muir Higginson, Noel Murphy and Ian Rose from the Donaghadee area of County Down, and they paid about Ir£35,000 for him and named themselves the Dee Syndicate. Two of them still keep a horse with Jimmy.

Monty's Pass went on to win six handicap chases including the Kerry National in Listowel, was placed in the Galway Plate and was second of twenty-eight in the Topham Chase over the Aintree fences. That came three short weeks after a hard race in Cheltenham, when he was fifth of twenty-one to *Blowing Wind* (remounted third in the 2001 National). He was barely home a week before he was off travelling again to Aintree and put up a mighty

performance. The Grand National began to look a realistic option.

Jimmy said to the owners,

'We will be back next year – for the big one.'

Monty's Pass was kept on the go through the summer, running well in May, June, July and August before winning the Kerry National in Listowel in September, and one more run in October, ridden in all of these races by Barry Geraghty. Then he was rested until March when he had two prep runs for Aintree over hurdles.

The ground for the National was perfect and Barry Geraghty had great confidence in his horse.

A full house of forty went to the start, several with excellent credentials, five of them vying for favouritism. Trevor Hemmings was trying with *Chives* and *Goguenard* and J.P. McManus was represented by *Youlneverwalkalone*. In the end, Ruby Walsh's choice of *Shotgun Willy* over *Ad Hoc* for Paul Nicholls saw him start favourite at 7-1; Tony McCoy picked the seven-year-old *Iris Bleu* who started at 8-1 along with *Youlneverwalkalone* (Conor O'Dwyer); *Ad Hoc* (Paul Carberry) was 9-1: the top four in the betting all ridden by top Irish jockeys.

But there was another Irish jockey riding on a high. Barry Geraghty had just ridden five winners at the Cheltenham NH Festival – and the money was pouring in on his mount, *Monty's Pass*, bringing his price down from 66-1 a few days before the race to start at 16-1. Mick Futter and his pals stood to win nearly £1million should he win, to go with their share of the winner's £348,000 purse.

Barry Geraghty hails from a farming and point-to-pointing family from Pelletstown near Dunshaughlin in County Meath. His father, Tucker, trains a number of racehorses with a good few winners; his mother, Bea, runs a successful riding school; his grandfather, Lawrence, bred *Golden Miller*, the only horse ever to have won the Cheltenham Gold Cup and the Grand National in the same year. *L'Escargot* achieved both wins, but with a few years in between.

Lawrence Geraghty sold the bay by *Goldcourt* out of *Miller's Pride* as a yearling for £100 in Dublin Sales to Paddy Quinn in County Tipperary; he, in turn, sold him to former amateur rider turned show-hunter exhibitor par excellence, Nat Galway-Greer, and from there he was sold to English trainer Basil Briscoe for £500. One of Briscoe's owners, Philip Carr, bought him for £1,000 and found immediate success as *Golden Miller* won three races and placed in his other four. So Philip Carr had much to look forward to, but sadly he became terminally ill and so *Golden Miller* was sold once again, this time to the redoubtable Dorothy Paget who in the same deal also bought future Champion Hurdle winner, *Insurance*, the two of them together costing £1,200.

Before long *Golden Miller* bestrode the NH world like a colossus. He is the only horse ever to have won five Cheltenham Gold Cups (*Arkle* won the three that he contested, but then broke a bone in his foot at Kempton and could not attempt the same feat.) Some of *Golden Miller*'s Cheltenham battles and wins were as good as National Hunt racing gets, but his attempts at Aintree were much more mixed. He first contested it in 1933 as a six-year-old, hot on the heels of his second Cheltenham Gold Cup win. Not surprisingly, he was all the rage; apart from the Gold Cup he had also won all four of his other starts that season and his trainer Basil Briscoe from Suffolk had him 'spot on' for Liverpool.

All went well on the first circuit, but jockey Ted Leader had to survive a monumental blunder at the second Becher's, then only two fences later, turning sharply at the Canal Turn, 'The Miller' dumped his rider on to the turf. Victory went to *Kellsboro Jack*.

A year later, 1934, found *The Miller* only second favourite, but despite this it was his year. Ridden this time by Gerry Wilson, and against formidable opponents including his

Cheltenham dueller *Thomond II* (who carried 12st 4lb to *Miller*'s 12st 2lb), he joined the front rank on the final circuit. Several horses were together clearing the last Valentines and coming to the final fence it looked like a fight between *Golden Miller* and *Delaneige*, but from there on one of history's greatest steeplechasers produced a turn of foot that quickly saw him go lengths ahead to gallop home in a then record time.

There must have been many fans who wondered whether they would now see a string of National wins from their hero, but unfortunately things went against him.

In 1935, at the incredibly short odds for the National of 2-1 (the shortest ever, though *Sir William* who won a precursor to the Grand National in 1838 was also 2-1, from a field of only three runners), the punters clearly thought *Golden Miller* unbeatable, even with thirty of the world's most formidable fences ahead of him; it was not to be. Towards the end of the first circuit, *Golden Miller* fell. *Reynoldstown*, yet another Irish bred horse, won the race for owner and trainer Major Noel Furlong, ridden by his son, Frank. *Reynoldstown* was to become only the seventh dual winner the following year when ridden by Fulke Walwyn, subsequently a top trainer; Frank Furlong was with his Regiment; he was later to be killed in World War II.

OPPOSITE: *Full flight in the 2002 Grand National;* Monty's Pass *leads the way.*
BELOW: *Winner's Enclosure and smiles all round: Mary Mangan, Barry Geraghty and Jimmy Mangan with* Monty's Pass.

In 1936 *Golden Miller* was with another trainer, Owen Anthony, because of events at Aintree the previous year; after *Golden Miller*'s fall Miss Paget had insisted on turning out again the day after the 1935 National, only for *Golden Miller* to unseat his rider once more, this time at the first fence. Sadly, in what would appear a fit of pique, she moved not only her star, but also all her other horses from Basil Briscoe.

Now, in 1936 and trained by Owen Anthony, *Golden Miller* was brought down at the first fence; he was remounted and, way behind the other runners, he doggedly refused a later open ditch; it was an ignominious sight so soon after his incredible fifth Gold Cup. 1937 was no better; *Golden Miller* displayed a very firm 'no thank you' to any more Aintree forays.

It is not for the National that Golden Miller should be remembered, but for his amazing Cheltenham record.

There is a plaque to *Golden Miller* on the wall of the stable where he was born, and there is a Golden Miller restaurant in Caffrey's pub at nearby Batterstown. It is no surprise

that all of the Geraghty family are involved one way or another with horses; the eldest son, Ross, is also a good NH jockey; Norman is a farrier, shoeing the high class inmates of both Noel Meade's and Tom Taaffe's stables; next comes Barry who lives nearby with Paula and their young daughter. Sacha is a journalist with the prestigious *Irish Field*; Jilly, rides in point-to-points; and the youngest, Holly, finds her sporting forte with camogie, the women's version of hurling and one of the most skilful of team sports. Along with their father they all hunt with the Ward Union Staghounds.

Barry's first win in England was in the 1998 Midlands Grand National at Uttoxeter on *Miss Orchestra* for trainer Jessica Harrington. He was seventeen years old at the time and still claiming (that is, receiving a weight allowance against more experienced jockeys); he rode the mare at 9st 9lb, a very low weight for a NH jockey, but on the way to the start the mare shied at a pram and Barry was unseated. However, in the race itself he rode beautifully. It was the beginning of things to come, for before long he was partnering Jessie's superstar, the Two Mile Champion Chaser *Moscow Flyer*. The partnership came apart a few times when the horse could put in the occasional monumental error, but for a number of seasons he was unbeaten when completing the course; his final record was twenty-seven wins and seven places from forty-five starts.

2003 was Barry Geraghty's year. Not only did he win the Queen Mother Champion Chase at the Cheltenham NH Festival on *Moscow Flyer*, but he also won the NH Chase on *Youlneverwalkalone* and the Pertemps Hurdle Final on *Inching Closer*, that one by a short head. He was crowned leading rider of the Festival and arrived at Aintree three weeks later on a crest.

The previous year's winner, *Bindaree*, was the only former victor to be trying again, but two others with form over the fences were Becher Chase winner *Amberleigh House*, and Foxhunters winner, *Torduff Express*.

Mick Futter and his fellow members of the Dee Racing Syndicate had less than ten minutes to wait to learn their fate: from the start *Monty's Pass* ran and jumped beautifully, handily placed and free from trouble. Poor *Goguenard* was knocked into by a loose horse and had to be put down; his owner, Trevor Hemmings, had also lost *The Last Fling* the previous year. *Youlneverwalkalone* was also injured, unable ever to run again, as altogether sixteen horses either fell or unseated. Several leading fancies were out of the race in the first circuit: *Chives*, *Youlneverwalkalone* and *Iris Bleu* all pulled up; *Ad Hoc* fell early on the second circuit and the favourite *Shotgun Willy* pulled up.

As they entered the final mile, *Tremallt* and *Torduff Express* faded; *Gunner Welburn* bowled along in the lead closely followed by *Monty's Pass*, *Montifault* and *Amberleigh House*. Monty jumped into the lead two out, jumped the last clear and, to rousing Irish cheers – not least from Mike Futter and friends – drew clear for a twelve length victory, *Supreme Glory*

running on for second from *Amberleigh House*, *Gunner Welburn* and *Montifault*. In sixth was the winner's one-time stable companion *Bindaree*, who recovered well from a blunder.

After the race Barry Geraghty said, 'The ground was right, the sun was out which he loves, and Jimmy Mangan had him spot on; everything fell into place and he gave me a dream ride, never putting a foot wrong.'

A proud Mike Futter spoke for the syndicate a few years later when *Monty* retired, 'He outshone everything in the parade ring – he was like a superstar going to the Oscars. He made other horses in the race, even the ones who were household names, look ordinary... His fantastic trainer Jimmy Mangan, his wife Mary and their loyal assistant Mossy were brilliant in producing the horse to perfection on the day.'

He added, 'I was delighted that many of my bingo punters in Belfast and Dublin won plenty of money on the horse.'

It was reported that the betting shop in Donaghdee had so many winning punters that they ran out of money.

Monty's Pass only ran in one chase before the following year's National, when he was seventh in the Kerry National, and in three hurdle races. But most importantly, at least to the Mangan family, was that, two and a half months after his National victory, he ran in

the one and only Flat race of his career, at his local Cork track, with none other than Mary Mangan in the saddle, making one of her rare race-riding appearances. It was the Paul Higgins Memorial charity race in aid of Irish Guide Dogs for the Blind, and all twenty runners carried 12 stone. Jimmy, with somewhere between one and two hundred career riding wins under his belt, also had a mount but, as he quipped,

'I didn't get the choice of horse!'

An event like this puts tremendous pressure on an amateur rider when their mount is world-famous but, just as Kate Harrington was to do on *Moscow Flyer* in a similar event at Punchestown four years later, Mary displayed nerves of iron, a cool head, and a polished performance, so that she assisted Monty to victory in his only flat race.

It was to be *Monty's* last win, but in the following year's National he finished a creditable fourth to *Amberleigh House*, carrying 18lbs more than he had the year before.

In 2005 he tried again, with Barry Geraghty remaining faithful to him, but while he maintained his 100 per cent record of getting round he could finish only sixteenth, and was honourably retired the following January. He now lives in contentment with the Mangans.

A few months after *Monty's* National win, Jimmy showed the various youngsters in the yard, mostly un-named, to the assembled Press. One was a full brother to *Silver Birch*, the 2007 Grand National hero. Another was *Conna Castle*, for whom his high hopes are materialising.

Meanwhile, he and Mary readily answer the door to tourists who see the village sign, and *Monty's Pass* happily poses for their cameras.

15

2005 – HEDGEHUNTER

THE 2005 TROPHY COULD SO NEARLY HAVE GONE to Canada with the name 'Kennebunk' engraved on it; that was one of five names suggested by family members to Niall Quaid, the original owner of *Hedgehunter*, a Limerick-man who lives in Ontario. '*Hedgehunter*' was the name he plumped for – most appropriately, according to trainer Willie Mullins. However after a string of near misses it was decided to sell him, it being a long stretch of 'pond' for Niall Quaid to cross to watch him coming second, again.

Willie Mullins thought enough of the bay gelding as a potential staying chaser to want to keep him in the yard; he contacted agent David 'Minto' Minton, who in turn contacted owner Trevor Hemmings. Hemmings had been searching for that elusive goal, the winner of the Grand National, for many years. He had had a dozen or so runners in the race and some bad luck; until then only three had completed the course and none had been involved in the finish.

Willie Mullins is top-drawer Irish racing. The eldest son of the legendary Paddy, he rode more than four hundred winners as an amateur himself and regularly wrestles for the trainer's

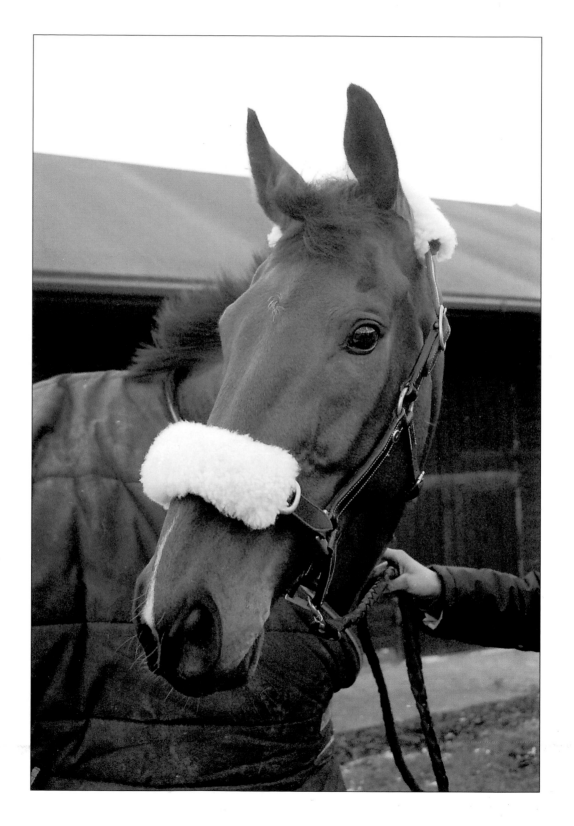

title with Noel Meade. He trains a hundred horses from his Closutton, County Carlow, home and does not plan to increase on that; his policy is to acquire quality horses that might win quality races.

The Mullins' house has, however, been stunningly extended since 2005 with what has been dubbed 'The Hedgehunter wing'. It is an example of just how life-changing an achievement winning the Grand National can be, even for someone already successfully at the top of the tree.

Willie and Jackie Mullins' son, Patrick, is following in his father's footsteps. At the time of our chat in 2007 the then eighteen-year-old had ridden twenty-one winners. By May 2008 he had become Champion Amateur and had ridden a life total of forty-five winners. At 6ft 1in tall, he plans to remain amateur. He tells an amusing story of his journey to Aintree the year of *Hedgehunter*'s win, as a fifteen-year-old pupil of Clongowes College, County Kildare. He and his friend, David Thomas, had to leave at 5 am in order to catch the early flight to Liverpool, but at that time the front door was firmly locked. Their dormitory was on the second floor of the castle.

Patrick takes up the story.

'We climbed out of the window and hopped down on to the swimming pool roof. From there we made it to the ground, just as the car that was collecting us crept up the drive with its headlights off.'

PREVIOUS PAGE: *From left, 03 winner* Monty's Pass,
Colnel Rayburn *and 05 victor,* Hedgehunter.
BELOW: *Jockey Ruby Walsh, trainer Willie Mullins and owner
Trevor Hemmings hold the trophy aloft.*

The driver was Willie's secretary, Katriona Murphy, sister of trainer Colm Murphy. Willie sits wide-eyed as he listens to his son's story for the first time, more than two years later.

'We had permission to go,' Patrick insists, 'but perhaps they hadn't realised we needed to be gone so early.'

It was not to be their last escape from authority on that memorable day. The lads roared their heads off as *Hedgehunter* stormed past the winning post, and they tried to run on to the course to greet him. They were stopped by security men, but made a dash for it and vaulted over the rails, laughing, cheering, screaming all the way, to greet Ruby Walsh and the equine hero.

Willie first came across *Hedghunter* in a batch of horses at Tom Costello's, he of the County Clare acres that are home to roughly four hundred young horses from foals to three- or four-year-olds, most of them 'pin-hooked' from the sales. Tom studies their pedigrees, but in particular he looks at the individuals; if he can foresee potential, he buys. When they are about three years old they are educated in a huge indoor school, and taught to 'loose school', that is jump without a jockey, starting over poles and progressing to a steeplechase fence, an impressive sight to prospective purchasers. Those that are mature enough will be sent to the Sales, while others will be broken in at home by Tom's sons, Tom and Tony, and begin their racing careers on the point-to-point circuit, Ireland's other big shop window. *Best Mate* progressed from two point-to-points while five other Cheltenham Gold Cup winners moved on from Costello's Newmarket-on-Fergus property via the sales.

Archie O'Leary, whose wife, Violet, owned Willie's flagship performer *Florida Pearl*, wanted a potential steeplechaser for his acquaintance Niall Quaid in Canada; a deal was done on *Hedgehunter*. In his first ten runs, *Hedgehunter* finished second seven times, including his first five.

He just wasn't 'sharp' enough to win a bumper and for Niall Quaid the sensible thing seemed to be to sell him.

Niall and his wife, Georgina Doyle, originally from Mullingar, County Westmeath, emigrated in 1953 when he was twenty and newly married; they boarded the SS Olympia for her maiden voyage – the MC for the week was Burl Ives – and of the hundred first class passengers they were the only fee-paying ones, the other ninety-eight all being on 'freebies'.

It was the couple's honeymoon 'and we've been on honeymoon ever since,' says Niall, 'we've had a lot of fun over the years.'

Niall's parents farmed near Limerick, the famous Garryowen rugby club (for whom Niall played) now being on what was part of their farm. His father bred a few thoroughbreds, one or two of whom won, and his sisters 'won ribbons in the RDS'.

His own love of racing stems from the 1940s with family visits to Limerick races and the local point-to-points.

'I was caught up in the whole atmosphere of horses, jockeys, shouting bookies and the racing throngs, which I believe are the most sporting party of all society and the most generous. I sincerely believe that jockeys are the best athletes in the world.'

He explains how, having been retired for some time, he finally became an owner.

'I kept a long distance interest in "home" racing, especially National Hunt, and I woke up one morning totally inspired to become an owner and wondered why I had not thought of such a brilliant idea before.'

Niall had the bit between the teeth and, after some phone calls and research, plumped instead for an un-raced bay four-year-old. Next came a family competition to name the gelding, the short list being Kilkee Date, Clare Wizard, Kennebunk (the summer resort in Maine visited by the family each year), Hedgehunter, and Late For Mass. Son-in-law David Halwig won with Hedgehunter.

Eventually *Hedgehunter* won a maiden hurdle, at his fourth attempt – and did so by twenty lengths! It was nearly the same when he then switched to novice chasing: two more seconds and a third before finally making it first past the post in an event at his local Gowran Park. Both wins were over three miles and connections could possibly have dreamt of a National at this stage, but the travel from Canada was difficult, and the close-down of racing due to foot and mouth, just as the Quaids arrived in Ireland for a three-week stay hoping to see one or maybe two runs, made it seem fruitless. In due course Niall decided to sell, and Willie put a deal together for Trevor Hemmings.

'If we had lived in Ireland we would not have sold him; we had three years of owning him and loved almost all of it.

'I have tapes of all his races and never saw him give less than 100 per cent, he was honest and brave. Tears flowed as I saw *Hedgehunter* run them ragged at Aintree in 2005.'

Hedgehunter's pedigree did not indicate stamina as a premium (he was by *Montelimar* out of a *Caerwent* mare), but when it came to jumping he was an absolute natural. It is doubtful whether connections guessed they had a horse capable of running *War Of Attrition* to 2½ lengths in the 2006 Cheltenham Gold Cup, for all that it was second again!

'Every time he jumps a fence he's looking for the next one,' says Willie, 'and no matter what type of fence you put in front of him, he adapts to it.'

These attributes had 'Aintree' written all over them. His programme now took him distinctly up in class, too; he finished fourth in the Hennessy Gold Cup at Newbury in November 2003 and third in the Welsh National at Chepstow at Christmas. He then won the Thyestes Chase at Gowran in January and did not run again until the Grand National, for which he was allotted 10st 12lbs.

At eight years old, he was young among modern National contenders, but all the signs were that this was the type of race for him. To those watching in the stands that year, 2004, *Hedgehunter* ran a blinder in the National. Out in front, jumping the fences 'for fun', he was running brilliantly for jockey David Casey, but used up too much energy for the 4½-mile grind. His jumping was so superb that it drew gasps of collective breath from spectators; he was attacking the fences with such enthusiasm.

Behind him, at the first Becher's, a number of horses were knocked out of the race as the result of interference from a loose horse; one who just managed to get over, jumping cleverly

from a near standstill, was *Amberleigh House*. Up front, *Hedgehunter*'s jumping continued to be superlative.

But going to the second last he began to tire, having led almost every yard of the way to that point; *Clan Royal*, trained by Jonjo O'Neill for J.P. McManus, was also running brilliantly, even at this late stage pulling hard under jockey Liam Cooper, and passed *Hedgehunter* here. 'J.P.', as he is known, is another owner who has been trying in vain for many years to win the race.

His luck looked about to change as his horse clearly had *Hedgehunter*'s measure, but then, at the last, he too ran out of steam. The next rival, *Lord Atterbury*, also tired and it was Irish-bred *Amberleigh House* who 'came with a wet sail' to win memorably for trainer Ginger McCain nearly three decades after the third of *Red Rum*'s famous wins.

Poor *Hedgehunter*'s reward for his courage was to fall at the last. He lay winded for agonising minutes; thankfully he then got up, apparently none the worse. But would it dent his enthusiasm for the challenging course?

The answer was to come in 2005. *Hedgehunter*'s 2004 run had shown the handicapper his aptitude for the course, while connections went without reward. He was certain to be burdened with more weight next year. Willie Mullins 'knew he had a realistic chance', and prepared a campaign designed to prevent that becoming crippling, so he ran him only in hurdle races through the 2004-5 season until after the National weights were out. He was allotted just 3lbs more than the last year, 11st 1lb. Willie then ran *Hedgehunter* in the Bobbyjo Chase at Fairyhouse in February, and won it. Aintree looked on target – so long as the horse had not been put off the place.

Saturday 9 April 2005 dawned with near perfect racing conditions. Willie and Jackie Mullins had arrived a couple of days earlier at the newly-opened hotel they had booked the previous Christmas. At that time Jackie had spotted an advertisement for it and asked Willie the date of the National.

The first Saturday in April, he told her, and Jackie made the booking.

But the date was April 9, the second Saturday in April, so when the couple turned up they were turned away. And by that time just about all of Liverpool was booked up; eventually they managed to find a room in a 'smashing place on the dockside'.

Now, *Hedgehunter*'s attractive Finnish lass, Miia Niemala, led him round the paddock that was electrified with anticipation for the great annual renewal. Her charge was 7-1 favourite ahead of a first in National history for the second favourite, *Forest Gunner,* was to be ridden by a woman, Carrie Ford, much the shortest price of any previous female-ridden runner. The pair were on 8-1, one point ahead of *Clan Royal*, 9-1.

The full quota of forty went to post and incredibly all were 'in the handicap', that is, had been originally allotted 10 stone (the minimum running weight) or more. When the first entries are made, usually somewhere in excess of a hundred of them, normally there are several in the 'extended' handicap, that is, below 10 stone and anything down to about 8 stone when clearly, the handicapper believes, they have no chance of winning. Incredibly, the lowest weighted horse in the 2005 Grand National was carrying 10st 5lb, 5lbs above the minimum weight.

In 2005 Ruby Walsh had the ride on *Hedgehunter*. Back in 2000, he had won on his father's *Papillon* when Willie's first runner in the race, Thyestes winner *Micko's Dream*, fell at the first. Trevor Hemmings owned another horse in the race, *Europa*, a 150-1 outsider trained by Ferdy Murphy, and finished twentieth.

This time *Hedgehunter* was restrained; he made a slight mistake at the tenth but was in no danger of falling; although there had been some early fallers, including *Lord Atterbury*, third last year, at the first, a record thirty-two runners completed the first circuit. *Clan Royal* had pulled his way to the front with the champion Tony McCoy on board but, in desperate luck, a loose horse swerved across him and carried him and *Clan Royal* out in front of the second Becher's. *Colnel Rayburn*, another Irish runner, was forced to jump it from a standstill, but got over safely and, enjoying a smooth passage down the inside, suddenly it was *Hedgehunter* in the lead, in company of half a dozen or so others in close contention. One of those was *Forest Gunner*, ridden with aplomb by mother-of-one Carrie Ford.

Hedgehunter was again jumping superbly and while it looked as if the others around him all had chances, Ruby had yet to push the button. He cleared the last nicely in the lead, just ahead of *Forest Gunner*, but both that horse and the other remaining runners ran out of steam, and as Ruby rounded the elbow he finally let *Hedgehunter* go. The response was so emphatic that he put fourteen lengths between him and nearest pursuer *Royal Auclair* at the line.

Patrick Mullins and David Thomas made their dash onto the course to greet them.

Celebrations continued long into the night, the next day and on into Carlow where horse and rider made a triumphant return, via parading to the delighted crowds at Leopardstown races.

It was early evening as locals began to fill the environs of the Lord Bagnal Inn, beside the River Barrow, in Leighlinbridge, expectantly awaiting the horsebox; at last it drew in, emblazoned in the race sponsors' John Smiths Grand National 2005 banner; quite the least perturbed being was *Hedgehunter* himself. Quietly he posed for numerous photographers, professionals and amateurs alike, as their cameras flashed in the growing dusk. Patiently he allowed himself to be patted, admired, and stroked. Ruby arrived and hopped on to his rugged back, and out came all the cameras again. This was the horse who only just over twenty-four hours previously had galloped 4½ miles at racing pace, crossed thirty of the world's most famous fences, stood inside his lorry stall on the ferry crossing, paraded round Leopardstown – and now this jubilant welcome home crowd.

At last it was back the few miles to the warmth and luxurious comfort of his stable – while the party rolled on long into the night inside the pub.

Meanwhile, across the water at her son's wedding reception in Windsor the Queen had, Niall Quaid recalls, announced first to the guests that *Hedgehunter* had won the Grand National – and only then had she got back to the subject of Prince Charles and his new bride.

That is not the end of the *Hedgehunter* story by any means. His route to the 2006 National took in a hurdle and three chases, including second to *Beef Or Salmon* in the Hennessy at Leopardstown and his first class run behind *War Of Attrition* in the Cheltenham Gold Cup. Willie had had no need to preserve his handicap mark this time for he knew it would be substantial following his marvellous victory at Aintree.

Once more *Hedgehunter* ran superbly at Aintree; left in the lead at the last Valentines it was only at the last fence that *Numbersixvalverde*, receiving 18lb, headed him and put six lengths between them at the post.

Hedgehunter's next season was interrupted by a knee injury, and although Willie finally got a hurdle race into him less than two weeks before the National, after a gap of four months, it was, as he says, not the ideal preparation for the marathon. In the race itself he suffered interference at both the second Becher's and Canal Turn; two fences from home he weakened, as up ahead *Silver Birch* ran out the third Irish winner in a row.

For 2008 *Hedgehunter* was twelve years old, not too aged for the National. He is one of those true Aintree specialists, where the challenge of the course brings out the best in him. He got around safely again and was then retired.

Hedgehunter's personality, says, Willie, is 'loyal, laid back, and very, very pleasant.' Said about a virtual member of the Mullins family it is the perfect reference.

16

2006 – NUMBERSIXVALVERDE

ON APRIL 8, 2006, A JOBBING BUILDER from Rhode, a small village in the Irish midlands, was paying his first visit to Aintree. A regular at the local betting shop, he decided the time had come to see the great race for himself, and he and three local friends took the boat over.

As the runners thronged out onto the course the stands were bursting. Paddy 'Whitey' Quinn found a spot, shuffled over a bit to let a man in beside him, and, of course, asked him what he'd backed.

'Well,' came the reply, '*Numbersixvalverde*, because he's mine.'

'Pull the other one!'

'No, I own him.'

'But you're in with the riff-raff.'

Bernard Carroll had been allocated three tickets for the owners and trainers stand, and had given them to his wife and two grown-up daughters, hence he found himself next to Whitey and pals, electrician Jim Hickey, shop and filling station proprietor James Murphy, and secretary of Rhode GAA John Glennon.

As the race unfolded owner Bernard Carroll could hardly watch, so Whitey gave him a running commentary. As the horse won, the men hugged and Bernard insisted all four of his new-found friends accompany him to the winner's enclosure. And to the Press conference. And to the celebratory drinks afterwards. Being shy himself, he even tried to push Whitey in front

of the television cameras when luckily his wife, Deirdre, and daughters, Roisin and Shauna, arrived to do so. But Whitey found himself feted:

'J.P, [McManus, Ireland's legendary racehorse owner] shook my hand, so did Lord Daresbury [Aintree chairman].

'Bernard Carroll is a totally down to earth gentleman, he'd only known us ten to fifteen minutes but he included us in everything.'

Bernard himself recalls,

'The hardest part was getting them into the unsaddling enclosure, we had to cod the police a bit, but from there on the racecourse PR man and other representatives were incredible, brilliant, and there was no difficulty including the boys in the John Smith's function and so on.'

The following year, 2007, for the horse's attempt to retain his crown, the 'boys' came over as Bernard Carroll's guests, everything laid on including entrance tickets and a meal the night before the race in Manchester. Whitey, for one, took up the offer of walking the course at 9am on the morning of the 2007 race.

He recalls, 'We were treated like kings.'

Bernard adds,

'The horse ran well again, to finish sixth, but weight is a great leveller. We'll try again in 08, he'll be twelve, but he only has a few miles on the clock, Martin has not over-run him.'

Bernard Carroll, a civil engineer who also has a business degree, is a builder and developer originally from County Clare. He first ran a racehorse in 1974, trained by Christy Grassick, and his first winner followed two years later, a mare called *Melody Music*.

Bernard recalls,

'She won a few races and then it turned out she was half sister to the Arc winner [Prix de l'Arc de Triomphe] and we sold her in Newmarket for £40,000, a huge sum in those days.

'I have been lucky all the way – better to be born lucky than good looking! It's all a lot of fun and a great way of getting rid of money!'

Bernard Carroll was one of Martin Brassil's first owners and has had at least one horse
with him ever since. Martin grew up in Newmarket-in-Fergus, County Clare, where his
elder brother John, a former professional jockey, now trains. When John went at fifteen to
learn his craft under Charlie Weld, Dermot's father, on the Curragh, the young Martin
had the pick of ponies to hunt and show-jump at home, and from this he progressed into

racing as an amateur; once, back in 1980, he rode at Aintree in a supporting race on Grand National day. Career-wise Martin first turned his hand to hotel management and began training in the prestigious Shelbourne Hotel, Dublin. But city life was not for the horse and country loving young man and he began working for various trainers. He served a considerable apprenticeship before setting out on his own as a trainer in 1994, including a stint of ten years with Mick O'Toole on the Curragh where he also rode as an amateur. After a decade there he moved on to Neil McGrath as head groom for five years, still riding as an amateur. But a bad fall and a shattered ankle in 1991 left him contemplating his future. His brother numbered Bernard Carroll, another Clare man, among his owners and Martin had sometimes donned his colours and won a few races for him. Now the owner – and loyal friend – promised he would also support Martin as a trainer and that, if he found a good horse, he would buy it for Martin to train.

So Martin, his wife Deirdre, and growing family moved to a yard at Dunmurray on the edge of the Curragh and trained just twelve horses. The first horse he bought for Bernard won a bumper, and before long he was winning with other owners' horses, both jumping and on the flat, including of a Listed race.

Numbersixvalverde was advertised in the racing Press, Martin saw him, liked him and bought him.

He recalls,

'I just loved his outlook; he had a nice step to him and that is what you look for in a horse. He wasn't over big, but had a nice bit of strength.'

At the time Bernard Carroll had just bought a villa in Portugal; he bought the bay gelding and promptly named the new horse after it.

As *Numbersix* progressed in his career, so did another inmate of Martin's small yard,

Nickname, who has turned into one of Ireland's smartest two-mile chasers on soft ground; he is owned by a Swiss, Mme Claudia Jungo Corpataux.

At the start of his career *Numbersixvalverde* was another 'nearly' horse: in his first eight runs he finished second no less than six times, until convincingly winning a maiden hurdle in Punchestown; several more placings followed and at the start of his third season he began chasing. After a few more placed runs in that sphere he won on a low weight in Navan, but it was his effort in the Thyestes Chase in Gowran Park, County Kilkenny, the following month, when still a novice, that he really leapt into the limelight. It was one of those horse-races that a non-betting spectator can only wish for a dead heat: right on the line nineteen-year-old amateur Niall 'Slippers' Madden snatched victory for *Numbersixvalverde* from *Kymandjen* who led for every yard of the three-mile race bar the final two inches, or short-head. It was the biggest win for horse, jockey and trainer – so far.

It put the horse into the picture for the Irish Grand National; he was Martin Brassil's first runner in the race, who secured the services of Ruby Walsh in the saddle, and from a high class field of twenty-six they won again, for an even bigger win in the trainer's career. Within a year, and with the Grand National now very much in his sights, he found his clientele had doubled to twenty-five horses.

Martin followed a similar route to other successful Irish assaults on Aintree by running

OPPOSITE: *Welcome home, hero!*
BELOW: Numbersixvalverde, *named after a Portuguese villa, and*
Niall 'Slippers' Madden, whose father 'Boots' was also a successful jockey.

his charge in a number of hurdle races as well as steeplechases, without winning. For the Grand National he was handicapped on 10st 8lbs; support for him began to mount. Martin, who mostly rides the horse himself at home, wisely had him schooled over a replica Aintree fence – courtesy of fellow trainer Ted Walsh – and, with Ruby Walsh naturally staying loyal to *Hedgehunter*, Slippers Madden, who had only turned professional the previous May after becoming champion amateur, had the ride; he couldn't wait. He had ridden his first winner just four years earlier at the age of sixteen and had never won a race in England. The betting had *Hedgehunter* and *Clan Royal* as joint favourites, followed by *Jack High*, *Innox*, and then *Garvivonnian* and *Numbersixvalverde* together.

Niall 'Slippers' Madden had the advantage of his father, Niall 'Boots' Madden, having successfully got round in the race when fifth on hunter-chaser *Attitude Adjuster* in 1988. So they walked the course together, and watched the videos, and dreamed the dream.

It was a first Grand National for the owner, the trainer, and the jockey. It went like clockwork.

Boots had drummed into Slippers the need to 'hunt round on the first circuit' (that is, not gallop flat out, go a steady pace); they were tactics that suited the horse, and his young jockey showed the necessary restraint to achieve it.

Not all horses take to the unique Aintree fences, but after four or five of them Slippers found 'the way the horse was travelling was unreal; he jumped brilliantly.'

Five horses fell at the first fence, including the previous year's runner up *Royal Auclair*, and while *Numbersixvalverde* remained near the back of the field throughout the first circuit it was *Ballycassidy* who led the way with *Puntal* close up. The big two of *Hedgehunter* and *Clan Royal*, Ruby Walsh and Tony McCoy, were lying in about fifth and sixth. Niall Madden, showing maturity beyond his experience, was not for hustling. Not for him the over enthusiasm or impetuosity of the young. Gradually, bit by patient bit, he allowed his willing partner to make up ground.

Turning for home, with *Ballycassidy* fallen at the last Valentines, there were six in contention. Between the last two fences Madden made his move, sweeping by leader *Hedgehunter*, burdened with much more weight than last year, and *Numbersixvalverde* galloped all the way home to win by six lengths ahead of last year's hero. It was almost a clean sweep for Ireland, with *Hedgehunter* a gallant second, *Clan Royal* a consistent third, and *Nil Desperandum*, trained on the Curragh by Frances Crowley fourth. The French-bred *Clan Royal* was an English runner, being stabled at Jackdaws Castle, Gloucestershire; but he was trained by Irishman Jonjo O'Neill, owned by Irishman J.P. McManus, and ridden by Ulsterman A.P. McCoy.

Rapturous scenes welcomed the winner, his quietly smiling jockey and charmingly modest trainer, into the unsaddling enclosure; handshakes, slaps on backs, cheers, interviews, TV cameras, photographs galore – and finally a jubilant singsong.

Slippers couldn't stay in Liverpool overnight for the ongoing celebrations as he was booked for a ride in lowly Tramore the following day – and he promptly won that, too; and then made it back to the Brassil stables for the bag-piped home-coming of his equine partner in their Aintree triumph.

In 2007 *Numbersixvalverde* finished a creditable sixth behind *Silver Birch*. Martin describes his star as 'a lovely, kind, easy horse with nothing nasty about him. I don't think I've ever seen him with his ears back.'

Of that day in 2006, he says, 'It was one of those great blessings in life.'

It was after the victory that Martin discovered a previously unknown family connection with the Grand National.

'My brother John and I thought we were the only ones interested in racing; I was only

seven when my grandfather died, but after the win we discovered that his first cousin, James Reidy, a dairy farmer of Rineanna, where Shannon Airport is today, had bred *Shannon Lass*.'

Shannon Lass ran third in Limerick for her breeder who sold her to England; James Hacket then trained her from Telscombe on the South Downs in Sussex for Lord of the Manor Ambrose Gorham. By the time she lined up for the 1902 Grand National she had already beaten 1901 winner *Grudon*, and the horse who was to win in 1903, *Drumcree*. Comparatively few mares go NH racing though strides have been made in recent years with mares-only races; but when a mare is good, she is often very, very good – and brave. *Shannon Lass* was one such and again, being a lady, was not one to respond to the whip; wisely, her rider, David Read, did not resort to one and she beat a good class field comfortably, with fourteen-year-old *Manifesto* carrying 12st 8lb into third place.

It is said that her winning owner, Ambrose Gorham, restored the St Laurence's Church and brought both running water and electricity to the village with his winnings. The winner's purse was £2,525; whether or not the owner had a bet on his 20-1 winner is not known.

He also left the whole parish in his will to Brighton Corporation with the admirable rider that it should find an incumbent who, preferably, 'is a sportsman and not a total abstainer from alcohol and tobacco.' Another version, however, states that he would not allow a pub in the village.

It is a quiet summer's evening meeting, bread and butter stuff, at the rural Irish Midlands course of Kilbeggan. A beginners chase is in progress; one horse somersaults at halfway and he and his jockey lie stunned for a moment. Then up they get, but the jockey is fiddling around the horse's head; he is picking mud out of the bridle and the horse's eyes; he strokes his face, checks the horse is ok and, with the remaining runners not far off approaching again, he remounts and jogs away.

Falls are all part of the job, but this also shows the caring side of the young man, Slippers Madden, the jockey who won the Grand National at his first attempt.

AND FINALLY – 2008 AND BEYOND

THERE WAS ANOTHER GOOD IRISH STORY in addition to *Silver Birch*'s in 2007. Trainer and former jockey Tom Taaffe, son of the legendary Pat and trainer of the 2005 Cheltenham Gold Cup winner, *Kicking King*, was having his first Grand National runner, a horse called *Slim Pickings*, a first crop progeny of a little known stallion called *Scribano*.

Owned by a sporting group of Kerrymen, the eight-year-old *Slim Pickings* had only joined Tom's Straffan, County Kildare yard in November. He fell at the last fence in his first run for him in the Thyestes Chase in January, but a good run in the Racing Post Chase at the Cheltenham Festival, in which he finished fifth, convinced jockey Barry Geraghty that he could run well at Aintree.

The owners were in mixed minds about it; for some people the Grand National is the pinnacle of their ambition, for others it is the height of fear. They decided to run. Pundits, playing on his name, put his chances as slim, and his price of 33-1 reflected the same.

The horse travelled over earlier in the week with head lad Shane Maloney; Tom was there on the Wednesday night for a dinner, coming home next day. He was booked to return to Liverpool early on the Saturday morning. On Friday night Tom's wife, Elaine, and their two young sons, Pat and Alex, set off for the 'lucky' holiday house in Wexford, where she was to meet more friends and family for a Grand National party. She wished Tom good luck and the boys excitedly waved cheerio.

Next morning, unexpected problems arose for Tom due to paperwork for his flight, the upshot of which was that he could not fly.

With his first runner in the Grand National at Liverpool, Tom was stranded in Ireland.

He returned to Straffan to make a string of calls: to the head lad, to the jockey, to the racecourse office to authorise someone to act for him; to arrange for someone to saddle up; to the owners. And, of course, to his wife. She was fatalistic about it.

'You weren't meant to go. Come here to the house.'

Tom could not promise for there was still so much to organise – he even had the owners' entry tickets with him – so Elaine did not tell the others about it.

Tom called trainer and former top jockey, Boots Madden, a relation by marriage; his son Slippers was trying for a second Grand National victory on *Numbersixvalverde*. He also spoke to Sean Byrne, Elaine's brother-in-law. No matter how good anyone else is, the finishing touch to a trainer's preparation of a horse for a race is the saddling. Tom's catch phrase, before letting the lad or lass lead the horse round the paddock is,

'You're good to go.'

It was little things like that that would be missing now, but of course the two men coped admirably with everything.

Twenty minutes before the 'off', Tom walked into the Wexford house, to squeals of surprise, dismay, disbelief … Meanwhile, at Aintree, the runners were off and running.

In Wexford, as the runners completed the first circuit, Tom remarked,

'Our boy is jumping well.'

The further they ran, the quieter the room became. *Slim Pickings* joined the leaders at the twenty-first; at the twenty-sixth, (the fence after Valentines), he jumped into the lead. The room was silent.

Then four-year-old Pat Taaffe yelled,

'Dad, he's winning.'

The blue and white checked colours were still in the lead over the second last fence. *Slim Pickings* and *Silver Birch* headed stride for stride towards the thirtieth and last of those formidable obstacles. They took off together, but *Slim Pickings* made a mistake, bad enough to halt his flow …

Patiently Barry Geraghty gathered him again and they set off in pursuit; he was just pipped for second to finish a brave and gallant third. For the owners it was as good as victory.

◆ ◆ ◆

A year on, Saturday 5 April 2008. It's a bitterly cold morning with snow and hail showers forecast, in contrast to 2007's heat wave.

The race favourite is *Cloudy Lane* who has won his last three races and is trained by Donald McCain, son of four times National-winning trainer, Ginger. At the last minute, money pours on to *Comply Or Die*, trained in Somerset by David Pipe, son of multiple champion trainer, Martin.

There is money, too, for last year's third, *Slim Pickings*. There's a heap of place money on veteran Aintree specialist and former winner *Hedgehunter*, who carries top weight. Next below him is another from Ireland, Michael Hourigan's *Hi Cloy*. Tom Mullins' *Chelsea Harbour* and his brother Willie's *Snowy Morning* are both fancied. Arthur Moore has *King Johns Castle*, a consistent sort with the inimitable Paul Carberry in the saddle; can a grey win at last?

Overnight one of the original forty has dropped out, allowing reserve *Dun Doire* in to the race; something similar happened before he won the Thyestes Chase for trainer Tony Martin – is this an omen? *Contraband, Point Barrow, No Full, Baily Breeze, Tumbling Dice* and *Black Apalache* make up the 13-strong Irish trained contingent. *Silver Birch* is not in the line up due to a slight leg problem.

Hopes are high for Ireland to make it an unprecedented four in a row.

For once there is a perfect start and all forty horses clear the first two fences, but then the spills begin, including poor Tony McCoy yet again as *Butler's Cabin* falls at the second Becher's when well in contention. Mick Fitzgerald, riding in his last National before retirement, takes a shocker as *L'Ami* crashes out. *McElvey*, second last year, was out of contention when he unseated his rider, Tom O'Brien at the twentieth; then, in a cruel stroke, had to be put down after colliding with a barrier when loose.

As they head for home led by *Comply Or Die, Hedgehunter* is showing his years; *Slim Pickings* and rider Barry Geraghty are enjoying another great round and look likely winners, but just fade to fourth. *Snowy Morning* is there, too, and fills third spot while stalking them like the proverbial cat is the grey *King Johns Castle* given the ultimate patient ride by Paul Carberry. On the run-in he looks sure to overtake the leader, but *Comply Or Die,* ridden by Irishman Timmy Murphy, to his credit pulls out even more at the end of the marathon contest for a deserved win.

Twelve-year-old *Hedgehunter*, who came in thirteenth, had run his final race, and retired after the 2008 Grand National. He'll live out the rest of his days on Trevor Hemmings land on the Isle of Man.

Though trained in England, the winner, *Comply Or Die* was Irish-bred and ridden. And Irish-trained horses finished second, third and fourth.

◆ ◆ ◆

It was an unduly cold May evening when Martin Dibbs, noting his mare was shortly ready to foal, turned her out in the paddock by his house, Clintown, near Mullingar in County Westmeath. This is his way. While other breeders have CCTV cameras and sit up all night when a mare is about to foal Martin turns his mares, eight in all, out to foal nature's way when they are ready. On the morning of May 9, 1999, he was greeted by 'a nice small foal' by *Old Vic*.

The dam was not called *Madam Madcap* by chance, 'she was a right handful', Martin Dibbs recalls, but she had foaled before and looked after the little bay colt properly now.